Sister Wisdom

Sister Wisdom

WOMEN OF FAITH, FORTITUDE, AND INSPIRATION

Helen LaKelly Hunt, PhD

ORBIS BOOKS
Maryknoll, New York 10545

Founded in 1970, Orbis Books endeavors to publish works that enlighten the mind, nourish the spirit, and challenge the conscience. The publishing arm of the Maryknoll Fathers and Brothers, Orbis seeks to explore the global dimensions of the Christian faith and mission, to invite dialogue with diverse cultures and religious traditions, and to serve the cause of reconciliation and peace. The books published reflect the views of their authors and do not represent the official position of the Maryknoll Society. To learn more about Maryknoll and Orbis Books, please visit our website at www.orbisbooks.com

Library of Congress Cataloging-in-Publication Data

Names: Hunt, Helen, 1949- author.
Title: Sister wisdom : women of faith, fortitude, and inspiration / Helen LaKelly Hunt, PhD.
Description: Maryknoll, NY: Orbis Books, [2022] | Includes bibliographical references. | Summary: "Inspiring portraits of women saints, trailblazers, reformers, and theologians from across the centuries and around the world"—Provided by publisher.
Identifiers: LCCN 2021052614 (print) | LCCN 2021052615 (ebook) | ISBN 9781626984622 (print) | ISBN 9781608339259 (ebook)
Subjects: LCSH: Women in Christianity—Biography. | Christian women saints—Biography.
Classification: LCC BR1713 .H795 2022 (print) | LCC BR1713 (ebook) | DDC 242/.643—dc23/eng/20211116
LC record available at https://lccn.loc.gov/2021052614
LC ebook record available at https://lccn.loc.gov/2021052615

Dedication

This book is dedicated to Mona Sinha, Sarah Haacke Byrd, and Amanda Griffin, the leadership of Women Moving Millions, a community of three hundred forty women in fifteen countries who have pledged a million or more dollars for women's causes. Their commitment to fund the needs of women, including the needs of some of the women you'll read about in this book, is helping to identify new solutions that can propel all of us toward a more equitable and mutually respectful civilization. Some have described the women in Sister Wisdom Book as trailblazers, and this is certainly true of the WMM community.

This book is also dedicated to Tracy Gary, cofounder of the San Francisco Women's Fund and the Women's Funding Network. She was my inspiration on the path that resulted in my personal funding to focus on women.

My final dedication of this book is to Maria Chrin, whose faith took her on a journey resulting in her being a founder of Circle Wealth Management. I've been blessed she took me on as a client almost a decade ago. She's been on the Board of WMM, but she is also such a brilliant support to me and my family.

The women in this dedication have helped women around the world, many of them marginalized, overcome prejudice and obstacles, and enabled their hopes and dreams for gender and racial equality come true.

Sister Wisdom can transform the world.

Contents

Acknowledgments

⁓

I want to acknowledge all those who have helped and inspired me with this project. I first want to acknowledge Robert Ellsberg, publisher of Orbis Books, who surprised me by taking on a manuscript I didn't think was yet ready for publication. In this time of such global chaos and unpredictability, when so many of us need more hope and inspiration, he shared my belief that these stories could remind the readers of the power of our spiritual practices to transform how we look at the struggles in our own lives, and the problems in our world. I acknowledge with gratitude Robert's guidance in preparing this book for publication.

One day Robert described the women in this book as trailblazers. This reminded me of a group of women I worked with who are very special to me: a community now called Women Moving Millions. These women were called trailblazers twenty years ago, because at the time, no woman who had access to resources had ever pledged gifts of millions of dollars to fund gender equity. With this funding, these women helped catalyze more justice and equality for marginalized women in society. Greater funding for those overlooked or disadvantaged is a prayer of so many of the women in this book.

I'd also like to acknowledge the visionary, courageous women in this book. They teach us that to achieve our goals, we must have faith in God's perfect timing. They have practiced never giving up, having faith, and trusting God's guidance in their personal lives. I, too, was shown "God's perfect timing" in the form of Robert Ellsberg! After writing these portraits so many years ago, Robert showed up just as the world needed to learn about these trailblazers, these Sisters of Wisdom, the most.

Introduction

Dear Reader,

This book has an interesting backstory. To understand it, I'd like to share some details about my life.

I grew up in the 1950–1960s, a daughter in a very wealthy family in Dallas. At that time, men and women had different roles. A woman's role was to become a wife and mother and create a loving home for her family. Wedding vows at the time typically declared that wives were *to obey* their husbands. In fulfilling this calling, my mother had been an outstanding example! She loved getting us all dressed up, so when Dad came home, he felt welcomed. A man's role, I was taught, was not only to be the head of the household but also to succeed in a professional arena and do something meaningful for society.

Experiencing all this, I wanted to break out of these structures. Why were women's talents and power confined to home life? Couldn't men share doing grocery shopping? I was determined to develop some sort of expertise and become smart enough on my own to contribute something meaningful to society. How I would accomplish that was a mystery. During my twenties and thirties, I kept reading psychology books and began to work as a feminist activist, supporting the idea of women's equality. But in 1990, something happened that turned my life in a different direction.

While living in New York City, I learned that a friend was hospitalized. Wanting to visit her, and deciding it would be nice to bring her a book, I went to a nearby bookstore. I usually went to sections on philosophy or psychology. But on impulse, I went straight to the section on spirituality. There, after quickly surveying the options, I impulsively bought a book by St. Teresa of Avila. This was a surprising choice, since I had been raised as a Baptist and had never picked up a book about a Catholic saint. I assumed this book by a saint would offer peace and comfort to my friend. During the thirty-minute taxi ride to the hospital, I began perusing the pages in the book. By the time I arrived, I had decided, shamelessly, to keep the book for myself. Instead, I bought my friend some flowers from a shop in the hospital lobby.

If I had supposed that the life of a Catholic saint was calm and peaceful, that was definitely NOT the life of Teresa of Avila. She was a powerhouse. She had the courage and audacity to confront her Carmelite order, convinced that they had abandoned the poverty and contemplative spirit of their origins. Against severe pushback and opposition, she managed to lead the "reform" of her community and went on to found numerous other convents. And then, with St. John of the Cross, she initiated a similar reform of the male branch of the Carmelite order. Again, I had thought that a nun's story would be about lighting candles and praying unceasingly. In St. Teresa, however, I discovered a bold life of spiritual adventure that had dramatic implications for her church and the wider culture. In reading about her life, I learned that it was her prayer life, her communication with God, that was the source of her power.

In the Southern Baptist Church in which I was raised, only men were allowed to be ministers or deacons and stand behind the pulpit. Women were not allowed to speak or pray from the pulpit, though wives could *walk behind their husbands* as they stepped up to make announcements or offer a prayer. But women had to stay silent. This all seemed normal to me at the time.

From Teresa of Avila, on the other hand, I learned that a woman could strongly influence her religious institution. And prayer itself could be powerful! This is not at all where I had felt my "source of power" would be. In the Baptist church, my prayers felt a bit structured and often passive. But Teresa's prayers seemed conversational. She sent a message upward to the heavens, and then she opened herself to receive a response. In one of her books, she described how a person can choose to develop a deeper capacity to be in conversation with God, to hear what God is saying. Over time, Teresa began to feel "instructed to help transform the church," so it would return to its original values, especially to learn what poverty can teach us. From Teresa, I learned that *being smart* isn't the way to make an impact, but rather finding and following one's calling, that is, God's unique plan for one's life. Might I also have a unique, preordained plan for my life?

Soon, I found myself buying other books about women saints. One day, oh my, I discovered Hildegard of Bingen! She was born in 1098 and raised in a Benedictine convent. She received visions, which she described in her books. She composed music; some became early versions of operas. She painted colorful images of the cosmos. She studied the medicinal properties of plants. She went on preaching tours. Today, one can still buy her music and read beautiful books that include her artwork. I began to read about these saints who received intuitive, spiritual, and/or artful messages that transformed their lives and the lives of those around them. And those messages were helping me confront problems I was facing in my own life. I began to read about other courageous, trailblazing women whose faith empowered their witness in the world. Not just Catholic saints. They were all around: Protestants and women of other faiths, activists, scholars, social reformers, poets, revolutionaries, and theologians—often sidetracked by history but hiding in plain sight. They invited me to see things from a different perspective. My goal became to develop my spiritual life, so I could then discover how to fulfill the life calling God had planned for me.

As an adult, my first marriage had ended in divorce. Oh, the pain. It felt like such a tragedy. When I met Harville Hendrix in 1978, he was a professor at a seminary at Southern Methodist University. He was also divorced. But he started giving speeches about "three stages of loving relationship," wanting to help people who fell in love learn how to maintain those feelings and stay connected. I had been praying for a way to help me to recover from the pain and sorrow of my own divorce. And here it was, in Harville seeking to help married couples learn to shift from conflict to connection. We decided to marry.

I was Harville's ideal *thought partner*, since I had earned a Masters in Psychology from SMU. I began to realize that out of my pain, my prayers were getting answered! I felt my heart opening. I began to realize, like the women in this book, that I was finding *my life's calling*, the assignment I was given to live with my life. Since then, my life has been dedicated to helping people learn to transform toxic relationships into connected ones. Harville and I feel that all of humanity needs to know more about how to be more loving to one another.

Here is the bottom line: No longer do I believe being smart is the answer to life. Instead, it's being truly open to listening and learning from our prayer lives; reading from scripture; and overcoming pain, struggles, and hopelessness from the heavens themselves. Also, the message I received from the Sisters of Wisdom, described in this book, was that we must treat all people respectfully; embrace diversity; and learn ways to be empathic for one another, even if we have differences.

Many of my feminist colleagues in the women's movement were skeptical about religion, based on the predominant role of patriarchal values and structures of authority, where women were taught to stay in their place. I knew that world. But through my reading about Teresa of Avila and others like her, I knew that there was another story to tell. On that basis, I wrote a book, *Faith and Feminism*, about five women of faith, whose vision and unwavering courage helped to transform humanity. I then decided to enroll in a PhD program at Union Theological Seminary.

The study of theology was surprisingly fascinating, due to professors whose theological perspectives expanded my worldview. I was inspired by the many books I read by feminist theologians and by the professors that I studied under. I think of these professors as saints, though they would tell me not to describe them that way! They were humble. But they were also passionate visionaries who emphasized universal inclusion and who believed love should be our global ethic personally and politically.

While studying under them, I thought of the life of Jesus. When he lived on earth, he spent time with the sick, "sinners," and other outcasts. He would also say radical things like "listen to the children," reversing the source of where wisdom resides. As I think of Jesus saying that, I remember pushing myself to get as "smart" as I could be, as if that were the apex of being human. Instead, Jesus spoke about associating with the marginalized, spending time with and even learning from those in need: my professors identified ways that society needed this kind of radical transformation. When seeking to honor a God of love, shouldn't we all be doing what we can to contribute to a civilization of love?

Being inspired by my professors, I began to realize they needed a much bigger audience. They became the inspiration for this book, which started with my writing a handful of "portraits of women" that I felt offered wisdom the world should know about. Each "portrait" presents a short biography of a woman and shares a spiritual concept or insight that might contribute to the reader's life. The number of women steadily grew, including historical and contemporary women, whose bold and courageous lives were rooted in the spiritual values they held and practiced.

I pray that these meditations might inspire you. And that their words will continue, now and into the future, to plant in our hearts the seeds of faith, courage, and hope. May the wisdom of these sisters light a flame in your heart, as they have done in mine.

Helen LaKelly Hunt

Queen Esther

⁓

Courage

I will go to the king though it is against the law; . . . if I perish, I perish.

It is never a good idea to base a relationship on a lie, especially if the man you're marrying banished his first wife from her homeland for being disobedient. Esther, a young virgin in King Ahasuerus's realm, had obviously never gotten this piece of advice. Her beauty won the favor of the all-powerful Persian King Ahasuerus. What didn't he know? Esther was Jewish, a race of people the Persians despised.

This story from the fifth century BCE has all the makings of the best reality show on television today—intrigue, banishment, and the potential for death. Mordecai, Esther's uncle, advised her to keep her lineage hidden from her new husband. Everything might have been fine, if male ego hadn't gotten in the way. Mordecai refused to bow down to Haman, the king's most important advisor. In retaliation, Haman convinced the king to announce a new law that would eradicate every last Jew in the Persian kingdom.

Hearing of this decree, Mordecai begged Esther to intervene—knowing full well approaching the king without permission was punishable by death. Met with her hesitation, Mordecai was given what might have been one of the few kernels of wisdom in his life, and said to Esther, "Who knows whether it was not for such a time as this that you were made queen?" Deciding to take the risk, Esther asked Mordecai to prepare the Jews to fast for three days and nights, and she would do the same. Afterward, she would go to the king and accept whatever fate befell her.

Terrified, Esther began to pray fervently. "O my Lord, help me who am alone and have no helper but You. For my danger is in hand. . . . Give me courage. . . . Put eloquent speech in my mouth before the lion." And finally, she prayed, "O God . . . save us from the hands of evildoers. And save me from my fear!"

Gathering her courage, Esther went to Ahasuerus. He looked so intimidating, however, that she fainted. Moved, the king rushed to help her, encouraging her to speak. Fortified by her prayers for strength, Esther was able to address the king. She asked him and Haman to join her for dinner.

On the second evening that the king and Haman joined Esther for dinner, she unapologetically revealed her Jewish identity. "If it pleases the king let my life be given me—that is my petition—and the lives of my people—that is my request. For we have been sold, I and my people, to be destroyed, to be killed, to be annihilated." When the king asked who had done this terrible deed, she named Haman, knowing full well he was the king's most trusted official. Moved by her courage and honesty, the king ordered Haman taken away.

The only thing that saved Esther from potential tragedy—not only alive but still enjoying her homeland and marriage—was her trust that God would answer her prayer and fill her with the courage necessary to own up to her omission. The enslavement of the Jewish people was wrong, and the righteousness of God was on Esther's side. Esther remains a beacon today because she is a reminder that every one of us is here to contribute something of worth that only we can offer. And the Jewish feast of Purim cel-ebrates Esther's courageous actions—actions that saved her people.

God, raise up the volume of Your voice, filling me with
courage and lessening the sound of my fears. Amen

Ruth

1200 BCE

———

Your People Shall Be My People

[W]here you go, I will go, and where you lodge, I will lodge; your people shall be my people, and your God my God; where you die, I will die, and there will I be buried. May the Lord do so to me and more also if even death parts me from you.

These well-known words are often quoted today at wedding ceremonies. Originally, however, they were spoken as a bond of loyalty and friendship between two women. Ruth's relationship with her mother-in-law, Naomi, models the mutual help through times of loss and transition. The Bible gives us no clearer expression of the value and importance of friendship.

Naomi, a Hebrew, had been living in the country of Moab. In Ruth's and Naomi's day, women were dependent entirely on male relatives—father, husband, or son. And so, it came that when Naomi's husband and both of her sons died, leaving her no children, she decided to return to her native Bethlehem. Before setting out on her journey home, Naomi told her two newly widowed daughters-in-law, Ruth and Orpah, that they could return to their own homes and remarry if they liked.

Orpah chose to stay in her homeland of Moab. Ruth, however, begged Naomi for permission to join her in Bethlehem. Naomi thought it best for her daughter-in-law to stay in Moab and return to her own life. She began to insist that Ruth do so. But Ruth had come to love Naomi as her own mother and wanted nothing more than to journey with her to Bethlehem. When Naomi finally agreed, Ruth began a daring adventure—a childless widow moving to a foreign country, where her Moabite race was not valued. For Naomi, the journey was a return to the familiar, but for Ruth it was a departure from everything she had ever known in life. Valuing the bond of friendship over the familiar, Ruth let go of her past entirely in order to embrace a future with Naomi and her people.

Ruth's loyalty and devotion to Naomi, and her complete embrace of the Hebrew faith, endeared her to Naomi's neighbors in Bethlehem. Her story is a beautiful example of the power of friendship, of how two women who care for each other can help each other through transition, difficulty, and pain. Ruth provided for Naomi and herself by gathering leftover sheaves of grain in the fields, and Naomi ensured that her daughter-in-law found a new husband in her adopted home. Together, with the strength of their bond intact, they began life anew, finding joy and comfort in a new land as dear friends.

> *My friendships are more valuable to me than gold, my Lord. Help me to listen, be supportive, and voice the love I have for my friends. I acknowledge Your presence in these very special relationships. Amen.*

Amma Sarra

———

Purity of Heart

*If I prayed God that all people should approve of my
conduct, I should find myself a penitent at the door of
each one, but I shall rather pray that my heart may be
pure toward all.*

Some of you may have heard of the Desert Fathers. Did you
know there were Desert Mothers, too?

In the early fourth century, many deeply spiritual women and
men began seeking solitude as a means of drawing themselves
closer to God. Leaving the cities, they went to live in the deserts
of Egypt, Syria, Persia, and Turkey—wild, remote places with few
sources of water or food. There, they believed, an ascetic lifestyle,
set in the raw presence of nature, would strengthen their spiritual
life and sharpen its focus. These desert dwellers came to be called
ammas and abbas, mothers and fathers.

Amma Sarra was an Egyptian woman who lived alone for sixty
years in the desert, first in a small hut, then in a cave by the Nile.
She devoted her days to cultivating an understanding of her inner
self and thus deepened her relationship with God. Some of her
teachings survive in ancient Coptic manuscripts.

Living in the wilderness, Sarra hoped that she would be able to
focus her whole being on God alone. It wasn't easy. She struggled
with what she called "fornication," by which she meant not only

sexual temptation but anything at all that took her mind away from God. Sarra never prayed that the warfare should cease, but instead that God give her strength. Because she recognized that the struggle was integral to her spiritual journey, she focused on keeping her heart open, enlightened, "pure toward all."

By better understanding herself, Sarra believed that she could better understand her Creator. In this spirit she examined her motives honestly. She asked herself constantly whether she was truly doing her best to purify her heart and treat others with the same love that God showed her. Doggedly she fought against the tendency to worry about what others thought of her and seek their approval. So, she practiced focusing on her inner life, "not that all people would approve of my conduct, . . . [but rather] that my heart may be pure toward all."

For Amma Sarra, finding true communion with God required her to experience the gospel physically. By dwelling simply, clothing herself modestly, and eating sparingly, she strove to share in Christ's humble relinquishment and thereby be drawn into His relationship with God. Caring for the welfare of others was the most essential step in this process. She explained, "It is good to give alms for people's sake. Even if it is done only to please others, through it, one can begin to seek to please God."

Her motherly wisdom, from distant centuries past, can inspire us today to align our external actions with our internal desires. Thus, we begin to walk a step at a time in Christ toward God.

> *Lord, strengthen my resolve in the spiritual battles I'm*
> *bound to have. Stay with me in the fray that I may*
> *resist being controlled by my own impulses or another's*
> *view of me. I long simply to follow in your steps—or,*
> *better still—to walk at your side. Take my hand. Give*
> *me your heart. Amen.*

Amma Syncletica

———

A Humble Spirit

Just as a treasure that is exposed loses its value,
So a virtue which is known vanishes;
Just as wax melts when it is near fire,
So the soul is destroyed by praise and loses all the results
of its labor.

Have you ever made a great effort to help someone else, and then been disappointed that effusive thanks and praise weren't forthcoming? This common spiritual shortcoming has been with the human race for a long time, evoking wise teachings about humility throughout the ages. Amma Syncletica, a desert ascetic, offered words of wisdom regarding this topic while living a simple, austere life in a tomb outside Alexandria, Egypt.

For Syncletica, there was a spiritual danger in the pride we feel when we master something. Expertise can foster a sense of superiority that destroys our sense of connection with and compassion for each other. Praise focuses our attention on what others think of us. Instead of focusing on being of service to others, we can become hurt or resentful about not being appreciated or praised enough. Pride can lead us to arrogance and feelings of superiority, when, actually, God calls us into humility.

"Just as one cannot build a ship unless one has some nails," Syncletica cautions, "so it is impossible to be saved without humility." She reminds us that the true gift of service is that, when humbly offering something of ourselves to others, we become God's hands, feet, or smile for someone in need.

When a good deed is done, it should be done with a humble spirit, not for the pride of the doer. And after mastering something, rather than resting at the top, Syncletica suggests that we circle back to the beginning. In this way, every mastery leads back into the humility of starting anew.

In fact, rather than focusing on the upward climb, Syncletica's words suggest that we could stay open to being curious—even vulnerable. Relationships grow when we stay open to others and respectful of their contributions. Only by surrendering our egos do we experience transformation in relationships. Emptying ourselves and developing the art of "not-knowing" prepares our souls for God to enter. "Choose the meekness of Moses and you will find your heart, which is a rock, changed into a spring of water." Quite a contrast—from a rock to water. A miracle, in fact. But then miracles are a fact of life in the world of Syncletica and the other Great Desert Ammas.

> *God, forgive me for resentful feelings when others don't*
> *appreciate me. Replace my resentment and pride with*
> *a sense of wonder of the other, and empathy for them,*
> *so I can experience the joy of Your Love in all that I do.*
> *Amen.*

Amma Theodora

———

Patience

It is good to live in peace, for the wise [person] practices perpetual prayer.

It was in the austere Egyptian desert, where a constant wind sifts through millions of tiny particles of sand, that Amma Theodora sought refuge from the world's temptations. There she prayed, preached, and awaited the kingdom of heaven. A fourth-century amma, probably the abbess of a small community of women, she was responsible for their spiritual guidance.

Mindful of the cycle of the seasons, Theodora saw the variety of human emotions as rites of passage that can bring us closer to God. "Just as the trees, if they have not stood before the winter's storms cannot bear fruit," she explained, "so it is with us; this present age is a storm and it is only through many trials and temptations that we can obtain an inheritance in the kingdom of heaven." All of God's love is available to us. We need only stand through the storms.

Reminding us that no one can escape the trials of their own life, Theodora told the story of a monk who wanted to escape the monastery because of his many temptations. He was putting on his sandals when he noticed another doing the exact same thing. The other said to him, "Is it on my account that you are going away? Because I go before you, wherever you are going."

The difficulties in life signal the process of life itself. In Theodora's words, "You should realize that as soon as you intend to live in peace, at once evil comes and weighs down your soul. . . . It dissipates the strength of soul and body. . . . But if we are vigilant, all these temptations fall away." Each season has its place in the cycle, their reoccurring moments in our lives. If we weather the variety of experiences with faith, at the end, we find ourselves right at God's side.

As a spiritual guide, Theodora believed that "a teacher ought to be a stranger to the desire for domination, vainglory, and pride . . . but [s]he should be patient, gentle and humble as far as possible; [s]he must be tested and without partisanship, full of concern, and a lover of souls." She counseled her following to avoid arrogance. After all, she explained, "neither asceticism, nor vigils nor any kind of suffering is able to save. Only true humility can do that. . . . Do you see how humility is victorious over the demons?"

Like all good teachers, Theodora enlivened her spiritual lessons with a keen sense of humor. For instance, to teach self-control, she told a story of a devout man who was insulted by someone. Instead of retaliating in kind, he retorted, "I could say as much to you, but the commandment of God keeps my mouth shut."

In the blazing sun of the Egyptian desert, Amma Theodora saw no mirage, but her true self. From that clear vision, she shares an insight that, despite a seventeen-century gap, has relevance for us today.

> *God, teach me to weather the storms of life with*
> *patience and love. Help me remember that in enduring*
> *life's trials, I come to know myself as I am. And in*
> *knowing myself, I know You who have always known*
> *me. Amen.*

Fabiola

D. 399

———

Repentance

*To change one's disposition is a greater achieve-
ment than to change one's dress. . . . A virtue
that seeks concealment and is cherished in the
inner consciousness appeals to no judgment
but that of God.*

—St. Jerome on Fabiola

We know of Fabiola not through her own words, but through
St. Jerome's praise in his eulogy for her. St. Jerome was a monk
who is perhaps best known for his translation of the Latin (Vul-
gate) Bible. He wrote of Fabiola's sins and how society condemned
her, and also of her power to transcend her past and let God speak
through her life. Fabiola didn't always live a pristine life, but she
was capable of remorse and of great generosity toward others in
need.

A fourth-century Roman woman, Fabiola divorced her first
husband and remarried. St. Jerome described her first husband as
being so horrible "that not even a prostitute or a common slave
could have put up with [him.]" When Fabiola married for the
second time, she unwittingly compounded her sins. Church law
prohibited divorce, and it also forbade a woman to remarry while
her first husband was still alive. After her second husband had died,

Fabiola realized the depth of her offenses and offered a heartfelt public confession. St. Jerome shared it at her eulogy, asking, "What sins would such a penance fail to purge away? What ingrained stains would such tears be unable to wash out?" He proclaimed: "As Fabiola was not ashamed of the Lord on earth, so [God] shall not be ashamed of her in heaven."

Fabiola's repentance involved selling off her sizable estate and using the money to assist the poor. She was among the first—and definitely the first woman—to found a public hospital in Europe. St. Jerome writes, "Often did she carry on her own shoulders persons infected with jaundice or with filth. Often too did she wash away the matter discharged from wounds which others, even men, could not bear to look at." Fabiola worked tirelessly for the sick and dying. We remember her not because she was always saintly, but because, as St. Jerome says, she underwent an inner transformation that expressed itself in acts of generosity and courage.

"She had mastered spiritual iniquities," offered St. Jerome, who admitted to many rebellious years in his own youth and who also had a true conversion. Inspired by the glory of Fabiola's life, St. Jerome reminds us, "But where sin hath abounded, grace hath much more abounded."

God, help me open to my own faults and find the opportunities for inner transformation that are all around me. Amen.

Hildegard of Bingen

1098–1179

———

The Fiery Life

Within every human being all things lie connected.

The life of Hildegard of Bingen blazed forth like a meteor in the dark ages. She was a powerful, innovative, and creative force. Imagine a woman today whose breadth of life work includes authoring nine books, seventy poems, several long musical compositions, and countless letters. Hildegard's interest in nature led her to become one of the first women medical writers to describe the female anatomy and explore remedies for common female ailments.

Now, imagine that all of this was done in the twelfth century, in an age where "no woman is to teach or have authority over men" (I Tim 2:12). And imagine, too, the audacity of a woman of that age who would rise up and challenge the head of the most powerful institution in the Western world. Speaking truth to power, Hildegard challenged the pope to wake up to the corruption in the church—where materialism and greed overshadowed spiritual devotion—and demanded that he set high standards for the clergy.

All of this work emanated from deep spiritual intuitions within her such as the conviction that all of life—God, nature, heaven, earth, man, woman—was meant to be eminently worthy and to be celebrated:

Human creature, take a careful look at humankind! Each human being contains heaven and earth and all of creation and yet remains one whole figure, and within every human being all things lie concealed.

For her, nature was an ever-present reminder that God was all around and within us: "O flower, you were not budded by the dew, nor drops of rain, nor the circumambient air, but divine light brought you out." Throughout her eighty-one years of life, Hildegard stayed focused on her ecstatic vision of life as an interconnected whole. She was able to call others into this vision so that they, too, could experience the world as divinely inspired and lovingly sustained.

> *God, open me to the divine energy that courses through all your creation and inspirits me as well. Make me mindful of the special place I inhabit in your world and the responsibilities I carry as a result. Amen.*

Telling Our Story

> *O fragile one,*
> *Ash of ash and corruption of corruption,*
> *Say and write what you see and hear.*

Struck down with a grave illness, many thought Hildegard was at death's door. As she lay prostrate, an inner voice commanded her to "Speak what you see and hear."

For Hildegard, this became a clarion call. She realized that, in being led to write down her own thoughts, she was becoming a vessel of God's voice. By recording her life story, Hildegard exemplifies the gift to society that occurs when we are bold enough to record the truth of our lives.

From childhood, Hildegard had experienced visions from God. At forty-two, she received a vision of such magnitude that she could no longer stay silent:

> And it came to pass . . . that the heavens were opened and a blinding light of exceptional brilliance flowed through my entire brain. And it so kindled my whole heart and breast like a flame, not burning but warming . . . and suddenly I understood.

In the fiery breadth of a single moment, this vision revealed the meaning of the sacred scriptures to Hildegard. God's truth, that all of life was one, interconnected whole, became the foundation of her faith. But it wasn't until Hildegard became seriously ill that she promised to obey the call and tell her story.

Engaging a monk to assist her by setting the words of her life down on paper, Hildegard found a renewed strength in the telling of her story. The act empowered her. Focusing the vast intelligence and divine truth that lay within her depths, Hildegard brought her work of reform, service, and inspiration to new heights.

> *Gracious God, give me courage that I may lift up my head, voice that I may tell my story, and ears that I may bear witness to the stories of my sisters. May our combined storytelling intertwine into an act of love that transforms the world. Amen.*

Marguerite Porete

D. 1310

Dying to the Self

For if one should take from this Soul her honor, her riches, her friends, her heart, her body, and her very life, one would be taking nothing from her, if God still remains hers.

Marguerite Porete was a laywoman and scholar from Belgium who believed that communion with God is possible through contemplation. Today, this is a faith practice many call mysticism. Little is known of her "ordinary" life, but her spiritual life is vividly illuminated in her book *Mirror of Simple Souls*, in which she explores a concept she calls "dying to the self."

In *Mirror*, Soul and Reason appear as characters in a play. Another character, Love, represents the path toward unity with God. The play begins by instructing the reader:

> Humble, then, your wisdom
> Which is based on Reason,
> And place all your fidelity
> In those things which are given
> By Love, illuminated through Faith.

The thesis, that God's gifts come through faith, stood in stark contrast to the rational principles of most writers of Marguerite's day. For Marguerite, logic inhibited a spirit-filled life: "For as long as I had you, Lady Reason, I could not freely receive my inheritance." This inheritance, of which Marguerite speaks, is immersion in the divine—a goal to which she dedicated her whole life.

Many clergymen were suspicious of this outspoken woman mystic who engaged in theological discussions. Her bold assertions represented a complete breach of fourteenth-century gender expectations. The clergy became even angrier because Marguerite placed the power to unite with God in the individual, rather than the church. And she underscored this radical belief by writing in her native French, rather than in Latin, the official language of the medieval church.

In 1306, church officials condemned Marguerite's book. They publicly burned all copies they could find and called Marguerite a heretic. She was soon arrested and brought before the Inquisition. When asked to recant her teachings, Marguerite refused. She was sentenced to death and was burned at the stake in Paris on June 1, 1310.

In spite of the Inquisition's attempt to destroy all copies of her book, several copies were hidden and thus saved. By the fifteenth century, *The Mirror of Simple Souls* had been translated into Latin, Italian, and Middle English. Today, her work is taught in theology classes around the world.

> *Compassionate God, may I remember Marguerite's courage in defending what she knew came from her oneness with you. Amen.*

Julian of Norwich

1343–1413

⌐

God Our Mother

*This fair lovely word "mother" is so sweet and so
natural in itself that it may truly be said of no one but
him, and of her who is mother of him and all of us.*

The fact that we don't even know Julian's real name is a sign of
the low status of women in medieval society. The name by which
she is known today comes from the church of St. Julian, where she
lived in Norwich. All we really know is that she was a middle-aged
woman who recorded a series of extraordinary revelations about
God's love for humankind.

Through these revelations, Julian found a space for women
within the male-centered theology of the medieval Christian
church. She envisioned humanity's relationship with the divine as
one of mother and child. Christ, the mother figure, nurtures His
human children with a parent's unending, unconditional, self-
sacrificing love. "The mother may give her child her milk to suck,"
she writes, "but our beloved mother Jesus feeds us with himself."

Julian elevates the act of mothering to something sacred. "To
the property of motherhood belongs natural love, wisdom and
knowing, and it is good," she claims. The image of a mother
breastfeeding her child mirrored divine love. "The sweet, natural
function of precious motherhood" for which a woman's body is

designed, appeared to her as an embodiment of God's sustenance of His creation.

Though church officials in her time deplored the female body as sinful, Julian claims that it has the potential to lift us closer to God. In her mind, the care and self-sacrifice associated with mothering inspire an imitation of Christ. By nourishing and sustaining one another, we physically reenact the love God has for us all.

And just as a good mother cannot help but love her children, no matter what, God's love for us endures forever. It is, Julian writes, "a love that can[not] and will not be broken by sin." Nothing we do can prevent God from loving us. Regardless of how frightened and ashamed of ourselves we may sometimes feel, God remains a steadfast, loving presence, waiting to welcome us back. As Julian reminds us, "our courteous mother does not want us to run away . . . Rather, he wants us to follow our childish nature; for when a child is upset or frightened, it runs quickly to its mother with all its might."

> *Lord God, by enfolding me in your loving embrace,*
> *give me the strength to enfold and nurture others, that*
> *we may all draw nearer to You. Amen.*

Teresa of Avila

1515–1582

Integrating the Shadow

What security can there be in a life as misspent as mine? . . . You would like to think I had been very holy. That is quite right of you: I should like to think so myself. . . . I cannot help having been what I have.

Saint Teresa of Avila insists on including the "account of my sins" in her story, "for it is just there that the glory of God is shown." It is surprising that Teresa would write so openly about her misspent life and her unholy living. But this is one of the reasons the writings of this sixteenth-century mystic continue to be relevant for us today. In fact, Teresa's books have sold more than any other Spanish author, aside from Cervantes.

Her spiritual autobiography charts the course of a woman we recognize, a woman who made false starts and took wrong turns. Her honesty about her faults and her riveting story of coming to Christ were pivotal in the conversions of two other saints who are featured in this book—Edith Stein and Dorothy Day. Teresa refused to dismiss her doubts and her errors. She knew her weaknesses were essential to her spiritual progress. They were, in some sense, her teachers. Her legacy lives on in many ways, including reformed branches of the Carmelite order, which exist today in more than six hundred houses worldwide.

So, what were Teresa's sins? Or, put another way, what was her shadow side, those parts of herself that she would rather have hidden? We can only guess from hints she left in her writing. She admits that when she was young, she was flirty, frivolous, rebellious, party loving, and boy crazy. But she also longed for a life of substance.

Teresa entered a convent at age sixteen, left, and reentered later. Frankly, she found the life of a contemplative to be challenging, if not boring: "For some years I was more anxious that the hour I had determined to spend in prayer be over, than I was to remain there, and more anxious to listen for the striking of the clock." This is an amazing admission from a woman who became famous for her books on how to achieve ecstatic union with God through contemplative prayer.

Her transformation from frivolous girl into spiritual leader occurred because she was able to accept who she was, shadow and all, and open herself to the miracle of God's transforming love. What was required were honesty and a simple desire to connect with Christ, the ultimate source of love and forgiveness.

Teresa drew on the totality of her life—her inner conflicts, her boredom and her persistent self-doubts—to inspire and reassure others. "If, then, you sometimes fall, do not lose heart, or cease striving to make progress, for even out of your fall God will bring good."

> *Merciful God, help me understand that all parts of me—including those that I would rather stay hidden—can be put to use in your service. As Teresa reminds me, "there is nothing for me to do but approach God and trust in the merits of His Son, and of the Virgin, His Mother . . ." Amen.*

Interior Castles

*I began to think of the soul as if it were a castle made
of a single diamond, or of very clear crystal, in which
there are many rooms, just as in Heaven there are
many mansions.*

The progression of the soul's evolution, as Teresa saw and shared
it, is a transformation from the suffering of attachment to the bliss
of complete union with God. Teresa used seven mansions in a
castle as the metaphor for this spiritual evolution.

For some of us, this progression begins as the dull ache of an
unnamable spiritual longing. For others, our willingness to take
the first step results from a traumatic or tragic event. Anyone who
has fought her way through the dark night of emotional pain and
survived to see the soft pastel dawn of a new day instinctively un-
derstands the soul's journey. As you ascend, you see the same view,
but from a perspective that keeps expanding. The first mansion,
"the mansion of humility," finds us in the basement. Though you
are in the castle, just as the soul is always in a state of grace, "so
many reptiles get in . . . [you] are unable to appreciate the beauty
of the castle or to find any peace within it."

In the second mansion, "the mansion of the practice of prayer,"
the soul is strengthened, often "through sickness and trials." It is
easy to feel victimized. But just as God tests us, God is also reas-
suring us. "And this voice of His is so sweet" that we recognize, if
only in a glimmer, that we wouldn't be so upset if our soul wasn't
yearning for complete union.

"The mansion of exemplary life" comes next, beginning with a
warning about the dangers of getting smug. This caution stops in
our tracks those of us who assume we can achieve any imaginable

height after struggling with and finally attaining the smallest win. As we "practice humility" we grow closer to God.

In the fourth mansion of "spiritual consolations," the hard work we've done is rewarded, because God has been infusing our soul. Whereas in the second mansion, we recoiled from being tested, we now desire trials because we "cherish a great desire to do something for God." In order to continue ascending the stairs toward God, "we should take proper measures and learn to understand ourselves."

In the fifth mansion, "Prayer and union" bring with them certainty of soul. "God implants Himself in the interior of the soul in such a way that, when it returns to itself, it cannot possibly doubt that God has been in it and it has been in God; so firmly does this truth remain within it that, although for years God may never grant it that favor again, it can neither forget it nor doubt that it has received it."

By the sixth mansion, resistance is gone, leading to a growing intimacy between God and soul. "Such a soul would gladly have a thousand lives so as to use them all for God, and it would like everything on earth to be tongue so that it might praise Him."

The last, seventh mansion, is union—or spiritual marriage—with God. Here, the soul dwells with God and the mansion of this marriage "may be called another heaven."

Ascending toward God is not for the faint of heart! In the end, however, Teresa assures us it is more than worth it, bringing "a spiritual sweetness much greater than we can obtain from the pleasures and distractions of this life." She assured the young women in her convents, "The time will come when you will understand how trifling everything else is next to so precious a reward."

God, I struggle with the same conflicts as Teresa. I
want what I want! But I also want what You want. In

*the dim light of my life and the utter darkness, please
help me to stay open to Your wisdom and love that are
so much greater than my own. Amen.*

The Garden

*There comes a time when the soul feels like anything
but a garden. Everything seems dry to it and no water
comes to refresh it.*

*This rain from heaven often comes when the gardener
is least expecting it.*

People in recovery are sometimes encouraged to purchase a
plant—just one plant. Because if they can learn to care for that
plant and water it regularly, they can learn to take care of themselves. Teresa of Avila understood that cultivating our spirits also
requires a careful, regular discipline. To illustrate this, she wrote
"The Four Waters of Prayer."

The Four Waters uses the orchard, or garden, as a metaphor for
the soul. Like a garden, if the soul is abandoned, it will become
an arid and inhospitable landscape. But when given the smallest
bits of attention—a time of solitude, or unrushed prayer—our
souls blossom.

What Teresa suggests in "Four Waters" is that cultivating spiritual discipline becomes easier over time. In the First Water, we
have to draw the water up from a deep well one small bucket at a
time. It takes a great deal of effort pulling the water out. And such
efforts "will mean advancing at the pace of a hen." But though the
work is hard, the soil begins to feel nourished.

In the Second Water, a pulley system has been erected, and the bucket lifts the water out with much greater ease. Prayer becomes more natural. It begins to flow more. The soil becomes more nourished. In the Third Water, a gardener appears who digs irrigation ditches. Now the garden can be nourished with more natural elements—a nearby stream, conduits, and gravity—to nurture the soil. By the Fourth Water, Teresa notes that sometimes grace appears. When you least expect it, there is simply a down-pouring of rain. And by no effort of ours at all, the garden becomes satiated. The heavens open, and we are flooded by God's love and deep peace.

The start of this process takes great discipline, however. It may take several starts and stops before the garden grows verdant from the rich, dark soil of the soul. Patience is needed. Yes, we may find one or two withered plants on our windowsill before we remember to water them regularly. Concurrently, it may take several attempts before we'll commit to a spiritual practice. Once we commit and are willing to do the hard work, however, God rewards our persistence by bringing an ease to the process.

Teresa suggested this gradient approach to the novices that came to her order. She assured them of the abundance of fruit that would result: "Those who want to journey on this road . . . must have a great and very resolute determination to persevere until reaching the end." Teresa knew, it was the willingness to keep going that is rewarded.

> *God of all things, I pray for courage. I pray for vision.*
> *I pray for the words to fight the injustice around me.*
> *May Teresa be with me in spirit as I try to stay awake*
> *in my faith. I am in gratitude for Your saving help.*
> *Amen.*

Anne Hutchinson

1591–1643

Making Plain the Pathway

[One] who has God's grace in [one's] heart cannot go astray.

Anne Hutchinson's story is one of such conviction and courage that she took the number one slot on Eleanor Roosevelt's list of America's greatest women. She is the earliest woman on record to lead the public fight for women's religious equality.

Born in England, Anne witnessed her father's repeated arrests for expressing his religious views. From this, Ann learned two important lessons: The church could be political, far removed from God's design for her. And one's moral responsibility was to speak the truth, no matter the consequences.

In 1634, the possibility of a religiously free utopia came to Anne in the form of the Massachusetts Bay Colony. Anne, her husband, and children made the perilous journey across the ocean to America. In the new settlement, Anne's skills as a midwife were valued as well as her theological literacy. Her father had home schooled her and taught her biblical scholarship. She began to offer Bible classes to men and women in the settlement. Word of Anne's reputation for interpreting the scripture began to spread. Men, including the governor of Massachusetts Colony, began attending Anne's weekly meetings. Eventually Ann offered classes exclusively for women.

Though it was legal for a woman to arrange small instructional classes for other women, leading larger gatherings was illegal. As up to eighty women would gather at a time, some men in the colony—including the new governor—grew jealous of her popularity and angry at what they perceived as undermining their religious hold. So, they defined her Bible classes as potentially explosive and illegal; and they accused her not only of treason but sedition and breaking the Fifth Commandment (to honor one's parents). With a wag of their finger, they admonished Anne that speaking out on the "fathers" of the church was the same as going against one's parents.

Anne believed that the grace of God, not our outward works, was the key to salvation. "As I do understand it, laws, commands, rules and edicts are for those who have not the light which makes plain the pathway." Trusting her relationship with God, she expressed that "having seen Him which is invisible, I fear not what man can do unto me."

Anne's faith empowered her to give spiritual sustenance to many. Her Bible classes are now considered the first women's meeting in the American colonies. Alternately, her fearlessness would serve her well, for these seemingly innocent classes at the time—which enjoy such notoriety now—eventually forced her to make a life-altering decision between the mortal authority of men and the higher authority of God.

> *God, with the courage of Anne I stand strong, trusting*
> *my intuition, knowing that I hold within me the*
> *divine spark of our voice, ready to serve and protect.*
> *Amen.*

A Higher Authority

You have power over my body, but [only] the Lord Jesus hath power over my body and soul.

In 1637, Anne was tried by a panel of forty-nine men. She was not allowed a lawyer. The controversial nature of Anne's meetings (deemed illegal as large gatherings of women), and her steadfast refusal to bow to what she felt were blasphemous charges, resulted in her being brought to trial.

Excerpts from the trial document include Governor Winthrop, who intoned:

Mrs Hutchinson . . . you have maintained a meeting, an assembly in your house that hath been condemned by the general assembly as a thing not tolerable, nor comely in the sight of God, nor fitting for your sex.

Gathering herself up with great dignity, Anne answered her accusers eloquently, quoting passages from the Bible in response to the charges against her. When she spoke, her voice rang out strong and clear, filled with the deep, moral conviction that there indeed was something wrong—not with her, but with the law:

I conceive there lyes a clear rule in Titus that the elder women should instruct the younger [Titus 2: 3–5] and then I must have a time wherein I must do it.

Amazingly, it was her response (and not the governor's shameful words) that were considered disrespectful. After failed attempts to "discipline" her, Anne was pronounced guilty for "heresy," and she, her husband, and their fifteen children were then banished from the colony. Her belief in the wisdom of a higher universal law was too challenging for the Massachusetts Bay Colony's religious tolerance, which, ironically, had been the reason for the settlement. She is remembered for the words she spoke after her banishment was pronounced in court: "The Lord judgeth not as man judgeth. Better to be cast out of the church than to deny Christ!"

Anne and her husband left Boston with their children, and settled in Rhode Island. After her husband died, Anne and her children were ambushed in an Indian battle. In 1911, a bronze tablet was erected on the site, noting her death in 1634, and that

> *Because of Her Devotion to Religious Liberty*
> *This Courageous Woman*
> *Sought Freedom from Persecution in New Netherland*

The repercussions of Anne's convictions live on long after her death. She stayed true to God's direction for her life and because of her courage, women across America can congregate freely today.

> *Loving Jesus, Anne Hutchinson was guided by your*
> *vision of universal dignity and equality. Make me open*
> *to that vision as well, and help me, like Anne, find the*
> *courage of my convictions. Amen.*

Mary Dyer

1611–1660

Together We Stand

Of whom take you Counsel! Search with the light of Christ in you.

Mary Dyer is one of America's most important religious martyrs. She and her husband came to Boston from England in 1635 in search of religious freedom among the Puritans. Twenty years later on a return trip to England, Mary converted to the Quaker faith, which was illegal in the Massachusetts Bay Colony. But her religious zeal could not be dampened by repressive laws. She made it her mission to minister to those who were imprisoned or otherwise victimized by religious discrimination.

As a convert to Quakerism, Mary preached the "inner light" as the primary basis of spiritual revelation—the presence and voice of God within our very selves. She insisted that men and women stood on equal ground in revelation, worship, and church organization. For her, this was a cause worth dying for.

Mary agreed with her friend Anne Hutchison's public statements that God spoke to individuals directly and not through the clergy. In 1638, when Anne was brought to trial for leading Bible studies, Mary stood at her side as Anne was excommunicated from the church and banished from Massachusetts Bay Colony as a heretic and an "underminer of the government." These beliefs threatened the Puritan male leadership, the understanding of men's and women's roles, and the male-dominated social hierarchy of the state. Both Mary and Anne, along with their husbands, moved to Rhode Island to practice their beliefs in greater freedom. They were told that if they returned to Boston, they would be executed.

But Mary refused to stay away. She returned to Boston determined to challenge the death penalty for Quakers. She was arrested numerous times for her views, for visiting with imprisoned Quakers, and for associating with known criminals. Finally, on May 31, 1660, Mary Dyer was sentenced to death.

Before she was hanged, she refused the prayers of the church elders, asking instead for the prayers of all God's people, true to her belief that each person was capable of receiving God's wisdom and praying from his—or her—own inner light. Her final words were of forgiveness and clarity of purpose. "I came to keep bloodguiltiness from you," she said to her executioners, "desiring you to repeal the unrighteous and unjust law made against the innocent servants of the Lord." The next day Mary was hanged on Boston Common.

Today, her statue stands on the place of her death with these words:

> Witness for Religious Freedom,
> Hanged in Boston Common in 1660
> "My life not availeth me in comparison
> to the liberty of the truth."

God of truth, give me the courage to stand firm and not go back on my word. Even when I seem to be abandoned, I am not alone when you are with me. Amen.

Jeanne Mance

1606–1673

Courage in a New Land

*There is nothing in the world that I would refuse to do
to accomplish the divine and all-loving will of God.*

The history of exploration in the New World is filled with the names of men. Women haven't captained ships or led expeditions to new lands. Women came later to build the new settlements, but they weren't in that first vanguard of discovery. There is one exception. Jeanne Mance, a deeply religious woman, was one of the founders of the French settlement of Montreal, Canada.

Jeanne grew up in the small town of Langres, France. Her parents were well-to-do and saw to it that she received a good education. They never expected her to earn her own living. They were surprised, but ultimately supportive, when Jeanne announced she wanted to become a nurse. Once she mastered seventeenth-century medical skills, she made one further announcement: she felt called to serve God, not in a convent, but by traveling across the Atlantic Ocean as a missionary to what was then called New France.

Jeanne booked passage on a ship that was to sail from Paris. Shortly before boarding, she encountered Madame Angelique de Bullion, a woman with a big heart and a vast fortune. Jeanne confided to Madame de Bullion her dream of establishing a hospital in the new land. Madame de Bullion was so impressed with Jeanne's vision that she agreed to finance the whole enterprise.

Jeanne's partner in establishing the new settlement was Paul de Chomedey de Maisonneuve. Paul became the head of the colony, but Jeanne's medical and organizational skills ensured its survival. In the early years, when the colony had less than a hundred people, harsh weather, illness, and hostile attacks threatened to overwhelm their efforts. Jeanne made the dangerous Atlantic crossing alone several times to plead for the supplies they desperately needed to survive.

Once the colony seemed secure, Jeanne was free to build her hospital. "God's will is the only desire and love of my heart," she wrote to Madame de Bullion, as the hospital was nearing completion. The Hôtel-Dieu de Montréal opened in 1645 as the first hospital in North America. For a time she was the only nurse there, caring for the sick and making ointments and medicines herself out of local herbs and plants. It was four years before other trained nurses were sent to join her.

Jeanne wrote about what sustained her through her dangerous journey into a hostile wilderness. She said, "[God's will is] my passion, all my affections . . . and my sole paradise." This most independent of women relied on her close communion with God for her passion and bravery.

> *Lord, give me the courage to explore and define new frontiers in my own life. And give me the foresight as Jeanne did to recognize those who would make partners for me in the work. Amen.*

Sor Juana Inés de la Cruz

1648–1695

Speaking Out

*My writing has never proceeded from any dictate of my
own, but from a force beyond me; I can in truth say:
"God, You have compelled me."*

Sor Juana Inés de la Cruz was on fire with a determination to
participate fully in the intellectual life of her age. The problem was
that in seventeenth-century Mexico, girls were not allowed to get
an education or voice their own ideas.

When her brothers left for the University of Mexico, she begged
her parents to allow her to dress as a man and go too. They refused.
Obstinately, Juana immersed herself in the books in her grandfather's library and became as well read as any well-educated man.

In 1664, Juana's family sent her to fill the position of lady-in-
waiting to the viceroy and his wife at the royal court in Mexico
City. Although she was a court favorite, Juana left after three years
to join a convent. Now, as Sor Juana, she avoided being forced into
marriage, and, more importantly, was now able to devote herself
almost entirely to studying and writing.

Eventually Sor Juana grew to be a highly respected philosopher
and author. Writing about her own, singular commitment to a life
of learning, Sor Juana attributed her persistence to God. "Neither
the reprimands of others (for I have received many) nor reflec-

tions of my own (there have been more than a few) have sufficed to make me abandon my pursuit of this native impulse that God Himself bestowed on me."

She was brave enough to engage in every kind of philosophical and theological discussion with well-known men of letters. And when a bishop challenged her by quoting Second Corinthians, "Let the women learn in silence," Sor Juana had a response ready. She wrote in her most famous work, *Respuesta*, that " 'Let them keep silence' was meant not only for women, but for all those who are not very competent." She argued that if women were to keep silent, "then how is it the Church has allowed a Gertrude, a Teresa, a Brigid, the nun of Agreda, and many other women to write?" She asserted that women in the early church were educated and were writers, a fact that supported a woman's right to self-expression. In her opinion, instead of being silenced, there should be a committed effort to educate young girls, using older women as teachers.

As long as Sor Juana had the support of the viceroy, she was safe from the threats of the Inquisition. When the viceroy was recalled to Spain, the threat became very real. After a lengthy examination, the Inquisitors confiscated her books, musical instruments, and scientific equipment. Sor Juana maintained silence until her death in 1695, but continued to write in secret. Her major work, *La Respuesta a Sor Filotea*, was published and celebrated after her death. Its subject, women's right to an education, was an idea that was centuries before its time.

> *Let me not take my gifts or my voice, Lord, for granted, acknowledging instead that they come from you. You are the source of my desire to speak my truth. Amen.*

Kateri Tekakwitha

1656–1680

Conviction

I am about to leave. I am going to die . . . Take
courage . . . Never give up . . . I will pray for you, I
will assist you, I will love you in Heaven

— Kateri Tekakwitha, upon her death

Walk up Fifth Avenue in New York City to St. Patrick's Cathedral and you'll be met with a surprising sight. Carved into one of the four sets of massive double doors, among well-known saints, is the incongruous image of a Native American woman. Her story is virtually forgotten today. Yet she was important enough to grace the doors of one of the most famous cathedrals in the world.

Kateri Tekakwitha, known as the Lily of the Mohawks, was born in 1656 in Ossernenon, New York, to a Mohawk Chief and a French woman he had captured. Orphaned at four, Kateri was permanently scarred and partially blinded by the small pox that killed her parents, and her childhood was marked by loneliness and constant illness. Through these hardships, though, she remembered the beauty of her mother's Christian faith and drew upon that strength, staying focused on her search for God rather than on her own suffering. Kateri's motto became "Who will teach me what is most agreeable to God, such that I could do it?"

Unfortunately, the very strength Kateri received from her faith put her in jeopardy with her tribe. They wanted her to settle down to a conventional life and tried to trick her into marrying against her will. She adamantly refused, explaining, "I have deliberated enough. For a long time my decision on what I will do has been made. I have consecrated myself entirely to Jesus, son of Mary, I have chosen Him for my husband and He alone will take me for his wife."

The stronger her faith became, the more Kateri was ostracized. She wasn't allowed to eat on Sundays because she prayed all day instead of working in the fields. In fact, opposition to her Christian ways escalated until her family threatened to kill her if she didn't reform. She told them she would rather die than abandon her faith.

Kateri's reward for her unflinching resolve came on Easter Sunday in 1676 when Father Jacques de Lamerville, a Jesuit missionary, baptized her, and helped her escape to a Christian mission near Montreal, three hundred miles away. Though her name, Tekakwitha, means "The One Who Walks Groping for Her Way," Kateri was obviously guided by the inner light of her determination. She understood instinctively that "It is in us that God wants to take up His dwelling place. Our souls are the temples that are most agreeable to God." When she died, her grave in Kahnawake, Quebec, became a pilgrimage site. The last words she spoke were "Jesus, I love You."

She was the first Native American proposed for canonization, and on June 22, 1980, Kateri Tekakwitha, the young woman who refused to give up, was proclaimed a saint.

God, may I find within myself the knowledge of my true path and the tenacity to follow it so that in some small way, I too, can inspire others as Kateri did with my determination. Amen.

Sojourner Truth

1797–1883

—

Claiming One's Voice

"Sojourner Truth" . . . why thank you God;
  that is a good name.
Thou art my last Master and thy name is Truth.
So shall Truth be my abiding name until I die.

Sojourner Truth was born a slave. Named Isabella by her mother, her last name became the same as her master, Hardenberg. Considered less than human, Isabella had been taught "that we was a species of monkey, baboon or 'rang-o-tang, and we believed it—We'd never seen any of these animals." To claim her full personhood, Isabella had to find her voice. God was her protector and confidant, guiding her from slavery into freedom, and naming her anew.

Isabella instinctively knew that it was wrong for people to own other people. In the predawn light of a new day, she walked out of her master's house. Closing the door behind her, she took the first few steps out of bondage and toward her new, free life.

A freed slave, Isabella cleaned houses to support herself. One day, while scrubbing the floor, she heard a message: "I am no longer Isabella." Placing the sponge she'd been using aside, Isabella rose from her knees and asked God for a new name. Soon, this new name was resounding in the depths of her soul:

The Lord [named me] "Sojourner," because I was to travel up an' down the land, showin' the people their sins, an' bein' a sign unto them. Afterwards I told the Lord I wanted another name, 'cause everybody else had two names; and the Lord gave me "Truth," because I was to declare the truth to the people.

Sojourner had her freedom, and her new name. It was time to claim her voice, so she could follow her calling to free her brothers and sisters. At her very first antislavery meeting, Sojourner took to the stage and opened her mouth, trusting that the words would come:

Children, who made your skin white? Was it not God? Who made mine black? Was it not the same God? Am I to blame, therefore, because my skin is black? Does it not cast a reproach on our Maker to despise a part of His children, because He has been pleased to give them a black skin? . . . Does not God love colored children as well as white children? And did not the same Savior die to save the one as well as the other?

This ebony-skinned woman standing six feet tall arrested the crowd's attention. The conviction and force behind Sojourner's words filled people with awe. The power of her faith in God transformed the meek young girl into a self-assured woman. The more Sojourner spoke, the more powerful her voice became.

God, I know there are ways that I feel enslaved. Give me the strength that will empower me to end my slavery. Let me feel each day my trust in and love for You. Amen.

God Revealed

Honey, I jes' walked round an' round in a dream.
Jesus loved me! I knowed it,—I felt it.
Jesus was my Jesus. Jesus would love me always.

Sojourner carried within her a deep and abiding pride in who she was. This pride, and her unwavering determination to fulfill her God-given mission, led her to do amazing things that didn't even occur to most of the notable white men of her day.

First, Sojourner had people take her photograph. Often. She called these images her "shadow," and sold them to fund her anti-slavery work. Across the bottom of each photo she wrote, "I sell the shadow to support the substance." Aware of the power of story, which could move crowds to free slaves, Sojourner had a friend write down the narrative of her life.

Her favorite story, of course, was how she escaped from slavery that day. She reminded her readers that tragedy struck her life at age nine. With one crack of the gavel, she lost her mother and was bought by the cruelest of masters. Sojourner began praying with all her might "to make my massa an' missis better." But God didn't seem to answer her prayers.

Sojourner had realized that she was praying for the wrong thing. God wouldn't change others based on her prayers. Instead, she prayed for help to escape. Given this direct request, God provided the time, an escape route, and her new name!

As a free woman, Sojourner settled into a comfortable routine. And one day, it occurred to her "jest as soon as everything got a'goin' easy, I forgot all about God." Not needing help anymore, she had stopped praying. "I saw I was so wicked." Sojourner realized, and once again asked God for help. Rather than being forsaken, God revealed His son Jesus to her in a vision:

> "I begun to feel 't was somebody that loved me; an' I tried to know him. An' finally somethin' spoke out in me an' said, 'This is Jesus!' An' the whole world grew bright, an' the trees they waved an' waved in glory, an' every little bit o' stone on the ground shone like glass; an' I shouted and said, 'Praise, praise, praise to the Lord!' An I begun to feel such a love in my soul as I never felt before,—love to all creatures. An' then, all of a sudden, it stopped, an' I said, 'Dar's de white folks, that have abused you an' beat you an' abused your people,—think o' them! But then there came another rush of love through my soul, an' I cried out loud,—'Lord, Lord, I can love even de white folks!'"

Jesus suffused Sojourner with a profound forgiveness—for herself and everyone else—even her tormentors. She traveled the countryside, attending meetings, preaching and singing on a crusade to end slavery. Her forgiveness enabled her to do so from a position of love for God and all people. Those who heard Sojourner could feel the righteousness of her cause and the love of God alive in her. Though she faced many angry mobs, she was never harmed. Everyone, even her opponents, could see that she was connected to God's love.

> *God, thank you for reminding me, time and again*
> *through true stories like Sojourner's, that all I have to*
> *do to feel Your love is be open to Your love. Amen.*

—

Breaking the Chain

*I have been forty years a slave and forty years free, and
would be here forty years more to have equal rights for
all. I suppose I am kept here because something remains
for me to do; I suppose I am yet to help to break the
chain.*

Sojourner Truth was filled with the conviction that "the Lord
has made me a sign unto this nation." Armed with the certainty
that "in Heaven, black and white are one in the love of Jesus,"
Sojourner walked across the land making sure that injustice was
"root and branch destroyed."

The abolition of slavery was only one of many injustices that
Sojourner felt compelled to speak out against. "I have done a great
deal of work; as much as a man, but did not get so much pay,"
noted Sojourner, who summed up the suffrage movement with these
simple words: "we do as much, we eat as much, we want as much."

Sojourner was in her late sixties when she tirelessly traveled
the countryside fighting for human rights. On January 1, 1863,
some news flashed over the telegraph wires. President Lincoln had
passed the Emancipation Proclamation. Sojourner knew she had
to shake his hand.

Father Abraham has spoken, and the message has
   been sent;
The prison doors have opened, and out the prisoners went
To join the sable army of African descent,
As we go marching on.

After contacting the White House, she got word that the president wanted to meet her. An appointment was set. The day she arrived at the White House and approached the Oval Office, the president had a small crowd in there already, but he concluded his business with everyone else so that he could have uninterrupted time alone with Sojourner. Upon meeting the president, Sojourner confided, "I never heard of you before you were talked of for President." Smiling, Lincoln replied: "Well, I heard of you, years and years before I ever thought of being President. Your name was well known in the Middle West."

By preaching against the sins of injustice, Sojourner gave people a chance to examine their values. By practicing God's law of forgiveness, Sojourner gave people an opportunity to change their ways. By choosing to hear and answer God's call, Sojourner helped secure equal rights for slaves, for women, and for all those who were thought to be less than fully human.

> *God, I recognize that Sojourner's ability to know Your truth came from her connection with You, a connection made stronger by her willingness to accept Your call. Please help me fight Your will less and accept Your love more. Amen.*

Lydia Maria Child

1802–1880

Fearless Sacrifice

All we can do is to work for the right with might and main.

In 1824, a young writer dazzled American readers with *Hobomok: A Tale of Early Times*. This historical novel dared, in a time when society regarded Native Americans as savages, to claim one of them as a hero. Lydia Maria Child, its twenty-two-year-old author, won instant acclaim with this book and went on to write many other popular articles and stories for children. Her body of work remains prolific and impressive. But even more remarkable was her decision to sacrifice popularity and financial success for her deeply held abolitionist principles.

In 1833, Lydia's career nearly came to a halt when she wrote *An Appeal in Favor of that Class of Americans Called Africans*, the first antislavery book in the country. Her admirers were appalled at the publication, but Maria had written and published the book with full knowledge of its inevitable consequences. "I am fully aware of the unpopularity of the task I have undertaken," she wrote in the book's introduction, "but though I expect ridicule and censure, it is not in my nature to fear them."

Although her book sales dropped and she lost her editorial post at a children's magazine, Maria stood firm in her position. She fearlessly condemned slavery for its contradiction of Christian teaching and insisted that it diminished both slaves and owners alike. Eventually she became editor of the *National Anti-Slavery Standard*, in which she explained herself:

> Such as I am, I am here, ready to work according to my conscience and my ability; providing nothing but diligence and fidelity, refusing the shadow of a fetter on my free expression of opinion, from any man, or body of men and equally careful to respect the freedom of others, whether as individuals or societies.

Despite condemnation from the South and conflict within the abolitionist movement, Maria continued to write boldly against slavery. Until her death in 1880, she held fast to her guiding principle: "Under all circumstances, there is but one honest course; and that is to do right, and trust the consequences to Divine Providence."

> *God of justice and mercy, guide me to the work invited*
> *by your love for humanity. Strengthen me to stand*
> *against the tides of prejudice so that in all things I may*
> *extend a hand of care and friendship to each and all*
> *your children. Amen.*

Standing in Between

> *I wish I could find some religion in which the heart*
> *and understanding could unite.*

Throughout her life, Maria, as she preferred to be called, was on a spiritual search. After rejecting the rigid Calvinism of her upbringing, she viewed traditional religion with skepticism. Still, her faith stood at the center of her life, and she continually explored the values of Christianity as well as other world faiths.

Maria both defended and criticized Christianity. Although she didn't always attend church, she advocated and yearned for social worship:

[M]y spirit craves it above all things. If I could only find a church, most gladly would I worship there. My soul is like a hungry raven, with its mouth wide open for the food which no man offers.

At the same time, she raised a prophetic voice against the church's hypocrisy, especially in the matter of slavery: "Alas, we carry on our lips that religion which teaches us to love our neighbors as ourselves, [but] how little do we cherish its blessed influence within our hearts!" Seeing the profound gap between what people preached and practiced, she was ambivalent about the church and would look for spiritual fulfillment outside traditional institutions. She said, "Most devoutly do I believe in the pervasive and ever-guiding Spirit of God; but I do not believe it was ever shut up within the covers of a book. . . . If we want the truth, we must listen to the voice of God in the silence of our own souls."

Despite this ambivalence about organized religion and her disappointment in its practice, Maria remained grounded in her spirituality. She hopefully anticipated a new kind of faith:

[S]omething is coming toward us (I know not what) with a glory around its head and its long, luminous rays are even now glancing on the desert and rock.

In the end, Maria had the courage to explore her questions and acknowledge the truth of who she was. Somehow her seeking didn't weaken her resolve; it strengthened it. "This standing between is painful business. . . . but as Luther says, 'God help me. I cannot do otherwise. Here I stand.' "

> *Gracious God, in all of my spiritual pursuits, help me to remember that You are bigger than any institution or religion. Help me to always put my true faith in you and then to take my stand. Amen.*

Maria Miller Stewart

1803–1879

A Woman's Voice

" 'Who Shall go forward and take off the reproach that is cast upon the people of color?' asked a voice from within. 'Shall it be a woman?' And my heart made this reply—'If it is thy will, be it even so Lord Jesus.' "

One fall day in 1832, Maria Miller Stewart stepped behind a podium and addressed a black audience, insisting that they had the right to US citizenship. " 'God hath crowned you with glory and honor,' " she thundered, quoting Psalm 8:5. "And according to the Constitution of these United States, God hath made all men free and equal. Then why should one worm say to another, 'Keep you down there, while I sit up yonder; for I am better than thou?' It is not the color of the skin that makes the [person], but it is the principles formed within the soul." The world was shocked to hear such strength coming from a black woman.

Maria's background had been unassuming; she had emerged from poverty. Orphaned at the age of five, she was taken in by a minister's family in Hartford, Connecticut; and there, she learned to read and write, which, combined with her intelligence and practicality, were the foundations of her shaping a public career and becoming America's first black woman political writer.

As a young woman, Maria married a prosperous free black

businessman, James Stewart, and settled into happy domesticity. But a chain of events occurred that radicalized her. James died in 1829, and Maria inherited his thriving maritime business. Almost immediately, the business was taken from her by a group of white businessmen who had worked with her husband. "In this very city, when a man of color dies, if he owned any real estate, it falls into the hands of some white person." She was left penniless.

Her anguish brought her to her knees, pleading with God to show her the reason for this injustice. God answered by giving her an overwhelming sense of mission. She then dedicated herself to the equality of women and the black race in America.

She wrote an essay against slavery that was published in 1831. She then published a collection of meditations, and delivered four public lectures between 1832 and 1833. She did so, even though it was considered most inappropriate for a woman to speak in public, especially a woman of color. But she insisted, "Did Saint Paul know of our wrongs and deprivations? I presume he would make no objection to our pleading in public for our rights."

And so, she became the first black American to lecture in defense of women's rights. "What if I am a woman; is not the God of ancient times the God of these modern days? Did he not raise up Deborah, to be a mother, and judge in Israel? Did not Queen Esther save the lives of the Jews? And Mary Magdalene first declare the resurrection of Christ from the dead?"

> *Oh God, I see Maria's willingness to be used by you. Guide me as I follow in the footsteps of those who earnestly work for peace and equality. Amen.*

Dorothea Lynde Dix

1803–1887

The Incitements of Hope

While we diminish the stimulant of fear, we must increase to prisoners the incitements of hope: in proportion as we extinguish the terrors of the law, we should awaken and strengthen the control of the conscience.

Dorothea Dix had to grow up quickly. Her father, a traveling salesman, was an alcoholic, and her mother was incapacitated by depression. Given both parents' struggles with mental illness and addiction, it is no wonder she spent her life taking on institutional reform.

Her commitment and career started when she volunteered to teach Sunday school to women inmates in the East Cambridge jail. What she saw tortured her. Imagine being assaulted by the sight of naked inmates crammed into soiled, iron-barred cells. That was the horror that took hold of Dorothea's life.

She began to act—and she did so in a time when women were not considered full citizens. None had the right to vote, few had jobs, and it was unheard of that they travel on their own. Nothing stopped Dorothea. She knew little about mental illness, but she believed that every human being deserved dignity. She also believed that improved conditions might open the door to recovery.

She began visiting institutions throughout the state of Massachusetts. After compiling data, she appeared before the state legislature, beseeching them to "exercise that wisdom which is the breath of the power of God." Dorothea's report opened with a summary of her life's work:

> I come to present the strong claims of suffering humanity.
> I come to place before the Legislature of Massachusetts
> the condition of the miserable, the desolate, the outcast.
> I come as the advocate of helpless, forgotten, insane men
> and women; of beings sunk to a condition from which the
> unconcerned world would start with real horror.

Her views on treatment for the mentally ill were radical, visionary, and completely on target. As she fought for reform and conditions improved, so, too, did patients.

After reforming institutions in Massachusetts, she took on the same task for every state east of the Mississippi. Then, after thirteen years of nonstop working, she decided to take a European vacation. She couldn't do it. (She resonated too deeply with the Unitarian belief of taking responsibility for the good of all society.) And the need energized her. She wound up spending two years in Europe repeating what she had done in the eastern United States. When you add up her works, the arithmetic is telling. Dorothea played a major role in founding thirty-two hospitals, fifteen schools, and numerous training facilities. Never one to let anything get in the way of service, Dorothea asserted, "I think even lying on my bed I can still do something."

> *When my sisters and brothers suffer, I suffer also. God,*
> *may every action I take contribute to the dignity of*
> *all human beings, especially those most in need now.*
> *Amen.*

Harriet Beecher Stowe

1811–1896

———

Stirring the Heart

It's a matter of taking the side of the weak against the strong, something the best people have always done.

Harriet Beecher Stowe, a devout white woman from New England, wrote a book that started a war. At least that's what Abraham Lincoln thought about the tremendous influence *Uncle Tom's Cabin* had in stirring antislavery sentiment.

Intent on galvanizing the mothers of America to rise up against slavery, Harriet created the character of Eliza, a slave mother, from her own experiences. She poured the depth of her own grief, losing her young son to cholera, into Eliza's anguish at losing her son on the auction block. Imagine how a slave mother feels, she implored her readers. Realize that slaves, too, are capable of crushing grief and paralyzing fear. What would you do if your children were taken from you to be abused and misused in another's home, and you were never able to see them again?

And you, mothers of America—you who have learned, by the cradles of your own children, to love and feel for all mankind, . . . I beseech you, pity the mother who has all your affections, and not one legal right to protect, guide, or educate, the child of her bosom!

The passage of the Fugitive Slave Act in 1850 pushed Harriet to write *Uncle Tom's Cabin*. The act made it a crime for citizens of free states to shelter or aid runaway slaves. So outraged were antislavery activists that Harriet and many others created the Underground Railroad to help slaves escape southern, slave-holding states and travel to the northern states and Canada.

Uncle Tom's Cabin, published in 1852, reached into the homes of ordinary people and showed them what slavery was like on a human level. They felt what it was like to be afraid all the time, to lose children who were sold like livestock. They experienced, in the depth of their soul, the hopeless rage of being owned by another human being. The book became a bestseller in the United States, England, Europe, and Asia, and was translated into over sixty languages. No other single publication did as much to fuel the fighting spirit of the North to victory.

Harriet believed that slavery destroyed the humanity of owner and slave alike. Still, she had to speak honestly about the slave owner's responsibility:

> I am speaking now of the highest duty we owe our friends, the noblest, the most sacred—that of keeping their own nobleness, goodness, pure and incorrupt. . . . If we let our friend become cold and selfish and exacting without a re-monstrance, we are no true lover, no true friend.

God of redemption,
You created me with the capacity for empathic understanding.
I am meant to feel the pain of others.
I pray for the courage to stay open, even when it hurts. Amen.

Elizabeth Cady Stanton

1815–1902

Determination

The best protector any woman can have, one that will serve her in all times and in all places, is courage; this she must get by her own experience.

The day her brother died, Elizabeth Cady Stanton's father—voice laden with disappointment—told her he wished she'd been born a boy, especially now that his only son was gone. Cut to the depths of her soul, Elizabeth vowed that she would be just as good as any man. Surpassing even her own determined goals, she became one of the preeminent forces of the women's rights movement in America.

Elizabeth graduated from Johnstown Academy with honors. She had been one of the few girls there, and her father forbade her to attend college. Jaw set in a solid line of determination, eyes a steely blue, Elizabeth insisted on additional education. Worn down by her persistence, her father grudgingly gave his blessings for Elizabeth to attend Troy Female Seminary.

Intrigued by the complicated logic of law, Elizabeth persuaded her father to let her work in his law office. Although she couldn't practice, she was free to read. As she pored over case books and statutes, Elizabeth was amazed to find that laws left women no rights at all. Outrage galvanized her determination. From that day forward, all of her considerable intellect and energy was channeled into overcoming this inequity. Driven by her absolute certainty that a woman's right to independence was gifted by God, she demanded that a woman be awarded the "full development of her faculties . . . [and] a complete emancipation from all forms of bondage, custom, dependence and superstition."

Sparks flew the day Elizabeth met Henry Brewster Stanton, the great antislavery activist and orator. Each, impressed by the other's passionate commitment to equal rights, knew they had found a kindred spirit. Their marriage ceremony did not include the word "obey."

For their honeymoon, the couple attended the World Anti-Slavery Convention in London. While there, Elizabeth was horrified to learn that women were denied seating at the convention. Standing outside the auditorium, Elizabeth met the already famous suffragette and abolitionist, Lucretia Mott. Becoming fast friends, they agreed that if a woman was to be considered a full and participating citizen of the United States "she must have the same rights as all other members, according to the fundamental principles of our Government." The two women walked the streets of London, deep in conversation about their concerns, and vowed to one day organize a women's rights convention in the United States.

God, I know that courage often comes from difficult experiences. Grant me the fire of Elizabeth Cady Stanton, that I may greet each day of my life ready to take on whatever challenges present themselves. Amen.

Clearing Away the Debris of Centuries

We can make no impression on men who accept
the theological view of woman as the author of sin,
cursed of God, and all that nonsense. The debris of the
centuries must be cleared away before our arguments
for equality can have the least significance to any of
them.

It was a "century of struggle," taking seventy-two long years of women's marching in the streets and hunger strikes, for women to win the right to vote. When Elizabeth saw that the political victory was close, she turned her attention to dignity for women within the religious sphere. As a result, she and a group of twenty women, known as the Revising Committee, began to compile a revision of the Bible, called *The Women's Bible*. Of their collective work, the women quoting Psalm 55:14, shared that "we took sweet counsel together."

Elizabeth was obsessed by the fact that man "allows [women] in Church, as well as State, but in a subordinate position, claiming Apostolic authority for her exclusion from the ministry, and with some exceptions, from any public participation in the affairs of the Church."

Throwing herself into focused study, "I began to read the commentators on the Bible and was surprised to see how little they had to say about the greatest factor in civilization, the mother of the race. And that little by no means complimentary . . . For several months I devoted all my time to Biblical criticism and ecclesiastical history and found no explanation for the degraded status of women under all religions."

There was expertise among Elizabeth and the Committee in Greek, Hebrew, and Latin scholarship. Together, they attempted to correct biblical interpretation that supported women's inferior position privately and in the culture. The introduction to *The Women's Bible* states, "One has only to re-read the Gospels . . . to realize that Jesus was truly a feminist, that is, one who believes in the equality of women and men . . . and that Christianity is an equal-rights religion. That the ignorance, arrogance, and hypocrisy of the Church fathers should have denied this equality over the centuries is a staggering thought."

In contrast to the image of a restrictive God, Elizabeth and her Committee helped uphold what they knew to be the truth of God—a warm, loving presence that embraced all in the interconnected whole that is the universe:

> that set the universe of matter and mind in motion, and by immutable law holds the land, the sea, the planets, revolving around the great center of light and heat, each in its own elliptic, with millions of stars in harmony all singing together, the glory of creation forever and ever.

> *Lord, I know that You are the fountain from which my faith and self-reliance spring. Be with me as I fearlessly make my own way in this world, rising to challenges with the courage that comes from knowledge of your love. Amen.*

Frances Jane (Fanny) Crosby

1820–1915

⁓

God's Guiding Light

Do you know that, if at birth I had been able to make one petition, it would have been that I should be born blind? Because when I get to heaven, the first face that shall ever gladden my sight will be that of my Savior.

Fanny Crosby was born in a one-room cottage in New York. Her father died when she was a year old, leaving her mother and grandmother to raise her. Though she came into the world with normal sight, she was blinded at six weeks old. A country doctor, called in to treat a slight cold in her eyes, prescribed mustard poultices. Tragically, this was a mistreatment that destroyed Fanny's sight permanently.

Being blind didn't upset her, though not being able to go to school, did. "My desires were to live for some great purpose in the world." How would she achieve her purpose without an education?

Fanny's grandmother became her granddaughter's eyes. She described the saturated colors of the day's end, the vibrant greens after the gray sheeting rain, and introduced Fanny to the Bible. An apt pupil, it is said that Fanny was able to quote from memory many of the Psalms, the book of Ruth, the book of Proverbs, Song of Solomon, and much of the New Testament.

Memorization was not the only gift of Fanny's keen and agile mind. At eight years old, Fanny wrote her first poem, capturing her enduring spirit:

> Oh, what a happy soul I am,
> Although I cannot see!
> I am resolved that in this world
> Contented I will be.
>
> How many blessings I enjoy
> That other people don't.
> To weep and sigh because I'm blind,
> I cannot and I won't!

At age fifteen, Fanny's mother was able to enroll her at The Institution for the Blind in New York City. "O thank God," Fanny cried joyfully, "God has answered my prayer, just as I knew He would." Fanny was a student and also taught there for many years. Early in her school career, the principal told her that she needed to stop distracting herself by making rhymes. Although she left his office in tears, she couldn't give up her gift! Poetry just flowed from Fanny's mind and heart.

"I seem to have been led, little by little, toward my work; and I believe our job is to cultivate such powers as God has given us, and then go on, bravely, quietly, but persistently, doing such work as comes to our hands."

Fannie became a prolific poet, who wrote up to seven hymns a day. One song featured her pride in her life story, based on God's power flowing through her:

> Perfect submission, all is at rest
> I in my Savior am happy and blest,

Watching and waiting, looking above,
Filled with His goodness, lost in His love.

This is my story, this is my song,
Praising my Savior, all the day long;
This is my story, this is my song,
Praising my Savior, all the day long!

God, allow me to submit to Your will, and not be blinded by imitations and setbacks. Use me for Your glory so that through You, I can accomplish miraculous things. Amen.

—

The Voice of Angels

That some of my hymns have been dictated by the blessed Holy Spirit, I have no doubt. I have sometimes felt that there is a deep and clear well of inspiration from which one may draw the sparkling draughts that are so essential to good poetry.

With eight thousand hymns to her credit, Fanny Crosby gave the world a legacy that will live forever. A model for overcoming life's challenges, Fanny not only reconciled the hardships in her life, but she was ultimately grateful for them as well. "It seemed intended by the blessed providence of God that I should be blind all my life, and I thank Him for the dispensation. If perfect earthly sight were offered me tomorrow, I would not accept it. I might not have sung hymns to the praise of God if I had been distracted by the beautiful and interesting things around me."

Everywhere Fanny went, people shared the inspiration and comfort they felt when hearing and singing her hymns. The story of "Safe in the Arms of Jesus," one of her most popular hymns, illustrates the extent of her inspired gift and popularity.

One day a friend dropped by Fanny's house. He only had a few minutes before catching a train, but he wanted a new hymn to capture the hearts and imagination of young people at a conference he was attending. He played the tunes he composed on the piano for Fanny.

After listening, Fanny told him, "Your music says, 'Safe in the Arms of Jesus.'" Picking up pen and paper, she wrote as he continued to play. When she was done, he had thirty-five minutes to get to the train. Fanny folded up the paper and placed it in his hand. As soon as Fanny's friend was seated on the train, he unfolded the paper, and read:

> Safe in the arms of Jesus,
> Safe in His gentle breast,
> There by His love o'er-shadowed,
> Sweetly my soul shall rest.
>
> Hark! 'tis the voice of angels
> Borne in a song to me,
> Over the fields of glory,
> Over the jasper sea.

The power of this hymn, inspired by God and channeled through Fanny in mere minutes, is illustrated in various stories. A train conductor once arranged a police escort for Fanny after learning she was the author of the hymn sung at his daughter's funeral. A diary records that a bishop sang "Safe in the Arms of Jesus," while being dragged to his death by hostile fighters in Uganda.

This is just one of many hymns that have such stories attached to them. Wherever Fanny went, she could reduce crowds of women, children, and grown men to tears and to faith. She believed that it was divine inspiration that allowed her to write as she did. She continues to touch those who listen to her hymns today.

God, there are ways I am far more blind than Fanny was. May I take instruction from her that my dependency on You can transform any condition I am facing in my life today. Amen.

Mary Slessor

1848–1915

⁓

Women's Dignity

When you think of woman's lack of power, you forget the power of the woman's God.

Scottish-born Mary Slessor's childhood ended the day her father gave in to alcoholism. Her mother was unable to support the family on her own, so Mary quit school to work at the mills. Mary's day began before dawn, ending long after dark. Still, she made time to read a sentence or two from old textbooks each time the mill machine made its rhythmic pause.

The only thing Mary wanted in life was to be a missionary in Africa. At twenty-eight, she applied to the Foreign Mission Board of the United Presbyterian Church. A month later, she arrived in the Calabar region of Africa. With little training, and even less worldly exposure, Mary began her adventurous journey.

Mary was drawn to the beautiful African women, who suffered greater oppression than Scottish women. The tribe valued betrothed or married women only, marriage was polygamous, and chieftains' wives were forced to throw themselves, alive, on the funeral pyre of their husbands. From Mary's perspective, her work and the work of her missionary sisters was clear:

The women of the Church [must] make the native woman something more . . . than a mere creature to be exploited and degraded by man . . . [W]e must create some industry by which these women may earn their living, and thus become independent of the polygamous marriage and open insult.

In response to this self-proclaimed charge, Mary helped found the Hope-Waddell Training Institute, which trained women in marketable skills "and thus not only the woman provided for, but the country be benefited."

Training women to work was only one of countless ways Mary helped empower the women of Calabar. Because the natives believed twins were evil, women who birthed them were banished, their babies left in the wilderness to die. In response to this atrocity, Mary gave shelter to as many of these innocent babies as her house could hold, raising them herself to dispel the notion that these children were evil. She also set about speaking her mind to the tribal chiefs.

"I spoke to them not as a white woman," Mary explained, "but as a mother, and said that they ought to take my advice and keep their twin mothers and children." Mary's logic and reasoning, combined with her conviction "about the relation of human life to God's creating" won them over. Long before Mary died, the practice of banishing women and exposing twin infants had ceased.

Though her plate was always full, whenever Mary felt anxious or overwhelmed, she reminded herself, "It isn't Mary Slessor doing anything. It is God."

> *God, help me to recognize injustice and help me access*
> *the strength necessary to do my part in making life*
> *better for others. Amen.*

Impossible Courage

To know Jesus means to love Him, and with His love
in our hearts we love everybody.

Although Mary Slessor stood barely five feet tall, she was a lightning rod of faith bringing the comforting warmth of Jesus's love to everyone she touched. "My heart longs for you to believe in Jesus, to walk in His paths, and to know the blessings of eternal life through Him."

The justice system that Mary encountered as a missionary in the Calabar region of Africa was as primitive as the darkest days of lynching in the United States. Prisoners were forced to drink poison or dip their hands in boiling oil to determine their guilt or innocence. Refusing to allow herself to feel overwhelmed, Mary put her life in God's hands: "Lord, the task is impossible for me but not for Thee. Lead the way and I will follow."

Mary won the trust of many in the village by joining them in many customs and becoming fluent in the native Efik language. One day, she was summoned by the tribal chieftain when his son was near death. When the son died, the chief sought revenge from an enemy village. The men and women from the village were captured and sentenced to death.

Mary knew she had to do something. But, much like opposing a king, those who opposed the chief could also be put to death. "Why should I fear?" thought Mary, "I am on a Royal Mission. I am in the service of the King of kings."

For days, Mary argued and negotiated with the chief, reading him Bible passages and preaching of Jesus's love and forgiveness. Finally, the chief relented and freed the prisoners. It was the first time in their history that human blood was not shed on the grave of a chieftain's family member.

Mary channeled the love of Jesus, treating everyone she met with respect. Due to her persistence, the practice of human sacrifice was abolished in the region. Mary died at age sixty-six, surrounded by many of the tribal community that referred to her as Ma or "The Mother of All Peoples."

God, when I walk with you I can do the impossible!
Thank you for the joy that fills me in your company.
Amen.

Sister Blandina Segale

1850–1941

A World Full of Hearts

*I wish I had many hands and feet, and a world full of
hearts to place at the service of the Eternal. So much
one sees to be done, and so few to do it. I have adopted
this plan: Do whatever presents itself, and never omit
anything because of hardship or repugnance.*

When Rosa Blandina Segale was but four years old, her family
fled revolution-torn Italy to escape persecution and settled in the
United States. Blandina had spunk and a sense of adventure. She
would later enter the Sisters of Charity and join their missionaries
out west. Her written memoirs offer a rare glimpse of one woman's
life on the frontier.

By train and stagecoach, the trip alone was challenging. Still
Sister Blandina had little patience for naysayers. When two men on
the train warned of the dangers she would have to face, especially
among cowboys, she was unperturbed and later wrote: "Mentally,
I was wishing both gentlemen somewhere else." Then, when she
finally did meet her first cowboy, she introduced herself as a sister.
He asked whose sister and she replied: "Everyone's Sister, a person
who gives her life to do good for others."

Only five feet tall and twenty-two years old, Sister Blandina
arrived in the southwest and began her work. It wasn't long be-

fore she ran into her next confrontation. A member of Billy the Kid's gang was shot in the street. Sister Blandina admitted that what he did to others filled her with "intense loathing, and I will candidly acknowledge . . . fear also." Learning that the doctors in town refused to treat him, she said without hesitation, "We shall do all we can for him." And when her patient asked if God would forgive his sins, she recited scriptural verses illuminating God's mercy.

Tensions mounted when Sister Blandina heard that Billy the Kid was coming to scalp the doctors who had refused treatment to his gang member. "Do you believe that with this knowledge I am going to keep still?" an outraged Sister Blandina asked. When he rode into town, she met Billy the Kid openly on the street. He greeted her warmly and offered to grant any favor she asked. Looking him straight in the eye, she requested that he not take revenge on the doctors. Out of respect for her, he spared their lives. (This and other exploits earned her the title, in an episode of the TV series "Death Valley Days," "The Fastest Nun in the West.")

Sister Blandina's courage proved contagious and her passionate commitment to others made life in the "Wild West" more bearable. When people offered to do things for her, her response remained the same: "No, child, not for me, but for God."

> *God of my journey, I waver. Accompany me*
> *toward constancy. Breathe on me wherever the road*
> *bends. Build a campfire in my heart so that, with*
> *unconquerable spirit, I may join Sister Blandina doing*
> *Your work in the wilderness. Amen.*

God Provides

I'm going to make the effort, and I'm sure God will do the rest.

A tiny missionary with a huge heart, Sister Blandina faced many a challenge in the untamed West. She did her best to serve the needs of small frontier communities in the spirit and tradition of the Sisters of Charity. With a small staff and little money, she built schools, hospitals, and orphanages throughout Colorado and New Mexico, where she worked with Archbishop Lamy, perhaps best known through Willa Cather's novel memorializing his death. Her outlook guided her action: give it your all and trust God to do the rest.

Like a Hebrew prophet or Jesus with a hungry crowd on the mountainside, she also knew how to multiply resources. One day, the cook at one of her orphanages told her that there was no food for the 123 patients, orphans, and sisters at the hospital. Smiling, she replied, "That problem will be solved in ten minutes."

Seeing the vegetables in Archbishop Lamy's garden, she "made one athletic spring and landed near the cabbage patch." In her own words, "Throwing over into our vacant garden at least two dozen cabbage heads, I did the same with each of the other vegetables, only in greater number, as the sizes were smaller. Then I went to His Grace's door and rapped."

When the archbishop answered, Sister Blandina told him, "I have come to make a confession out of the confessional." Asked what she'd done, she replied frankly, "Stealing, Your Grace. With never a thought of restitution, I dug up enough vegetables from your garden to last us three days." The archbishop, of course, gladly let her have what she needed, and sent over a package of coffee, flour, and sugar later that same day.

For over fifty years Sister Blandina met every challenge with faith. In addition to the institutions she built, she established what might actually be the first recorded system for socialized medicine in the Wild West. Those who could afford to pay were sent to private families for nursing care. Then, to subsidize hospital care, she invited every member of the State Senate to visit the hospital. Surprised by her directness and amazed by what she had accomplished, the Senate unanimously passed the Relief Bill that granted the hospital a modest monthly stipend.

With all she did for others, Sister Blandina had but one prayer for herself: "that God may give me the grace to endure, to persevere."

> *God, help me, as you helped Sister Blandina, believe*
> *more fully in your limitless and unconditional love*
> *alive within me. Fortify my spirit, enlarge my heart*
> *and move with me outside the boundaries of myself*
> *when I think I am overcome. Amen.*

Mary Jane McLeod Bethune

1875–1955

Giving Ourselves Freely

I feel Him working in and through me, and I have learned to give myself—freely, unreservedly to the guidance of the inner voice in me.

Twelve blocks from the US Capitol, a woman and two young children are captured in bronze. The woman is Mary Jane McLeod Bethune. The statue, cast in 1974, was the first erected to honor an African American leader and woman in predominantly black Washington, DC.

Born in Mayesville, South Carolina, in 1875, Mary grew up amid the confusion that characterized the Reconstruction South. Her parents had seventeen children—most of whom were born into slavery. When Lincoln declared all slaves free, Mary suddenly had the right to an education. "One day, we were out in the field picking cotton and the mission teacher came . . . and told mother and father [about] a mission [school] where the Negro children could go. . . . I was among the first of the young ones to enroll." She earned a college scholarship, then attended Moody Bible Institute in Chicago. Called to assist others, Mary returned to the South to teach.

"I had more of a missionary spirit," said Mary, "the spirit of doing things for others. . . . If any child had no shoes, I always wanted to share my shoes." That "missionary spirit" fueled everything she touched until her death in 1955.

At twenty-nine, Mary decided to leave her teaching post and open a school of her own. With $1.50 she'd earned selling insurance she founded the Daytona Literary and Industrial School for Negro Girls. The school began with five girls in a rundown house that Mary rented for fifty cents. One hundred years later, her fledgling project had become the Bethune-Cookman College, and more than twelve thousand had graduated.

Mary transformed the servitude of her early years into a lifetime of giving herself freely in service to others. Honored as an educational trailblazer and human rights advocate, in 1935, she founded the National Council of Negro Women. In 1944, she helped start the United Negro College Fund and became leader of the Women's Army for National Defense to support the war effort. The first African American woman involved in the White House, she assisted four different presidents and was influential in shaping President Franklin D. Roosevelt's New Deal economic reforms.

On this stately statue in Washington, DC's Lincoln Park, Mary Jane McLeod Bethune holds out a favorite walking stick, given to her by Franklin Roosevelt, to the youngsters at her side. They reach up to take it. Forever captured doing that which she loved most, this is Mary's legacy: giving all of who she was to assist others.

> *God, as I feel the presence of you in my heart I am lit*
> *by the inspiration of Mary Jane McLeod Bethune's life*
> *and give myself freely and unreservedly to be of service*
> *to others. Amen.*

Evelyn Underhill

1875–1941

⌣

Rivulets of Gold

[My work is] not in some mysterious spiritual world
that I know nothing about; but here and now, where I
find myself, as a human creature of spirit and of sense.

Evelyn Underhill was born in England, an only child of parents who were not particularly religious. But even as a young child, she felt a deep intuitive sense that a spiritual reality ran under and through the visible world. Just as the mining of stone contains rivulets of gold, Evelyn reminds us of the treasures to be found embedded in our human nature. Her life-long fascination with the mystical dimension of life has informed and enriched the lives of millions of her readers. By the end of her life, she had published thirty-nine books and had become one of the Western world's greatest authorities on mysticism.

In her writings, Evelyn offers her view of how our inner worlds are composed: "We are essentially spiritual as well as natural creatures. . . . Most of our difficulties come from trying to deal with the spiritual and practical aspects of life separately, instead of realizing them as parts of one whole." For her, our challenge is to adjust to the fact we are both in the human world while simultaneously transcending it. In addition, she reminds those who may not have strong spiritual intuitions, to "Expect God—however unexpected

God's outward form may take. And to receive God in every sight and sound, joy and pain.

In her book *Mixed Pasture*, Evelyn encourages those on a spiritual journey to find a balance between action and contemplation. She insists: "To give Our Lord a perfect service, Martha and Mary must combine." While Mary had wanted to listen to Jesus to absorb spiritual truth, Martha had been organizing to help make Jesus's insights manifest in the world. Evelyn is saying we need to unite both energies. She spent her mornings writing and her afternoons visiting the poor and providing spiritual direction to those who sought her out. She counseled people to root themselves in the "homeliest details" of their lives, and yet without sacrificing their true home in the sacred.

And so, Evelyn beckons us toward a right relation in life through the unity of the sacred to the mundane. We do not have to choose between the practical Martha and the spiritual Mary. She wrote, "The experience of God . . . is, I believe, in the long run always a vocational experience. It . . . impels us to some sort of service . . . and awakens an energetic love."

> *God of wholeness, may I find the courage to live both*
> *Mary and Martha as I embody both spirit and action*
> *in my life. Amen.*

—

Unselfing

We . . . as cells of the Body of Christ, are called upon to
be . . . channels of His mystical self-imparting.

Anglican Evelyn Underhill is credited with returning a mystical tradition of prayer and contemplation to Protestant Christianity. In addition, she was the first woman to lecture to male clergy in the Church of England, the first woman to lead retreats in that denomination, and in 1921 the first woman to be invited to give a series of theological lectures at Oxford University. She did all this without a formal theology degree—though she was steeped in the classics, spoke several languages, and kept abreast of current theology and philosophy.

Evelyn believed that prayer was the means through which transcendence occurred. She said that prayer was essential for our own "unselfing"—laying aside of ego and possessiveness—that is the process of sanctification. The greatest contemplatives reveal to us a world beyond individuality, a world that is "unwalled." By continually laying down the "hard barriers of individuality," wrote Evelyn, and deepening the "unselfing of your attentiveness—you are [able] to enlarge your boundaries and become the citizen of a greater, more joyous, more poignant world, the partaker of a more abundant life." There are, as yet, no limits to this enlargement of spirit, which we access through losing our old self and gaining our new life through prayer.

Prayer is two-sided, both passive and active. Passive prayer is the internal contemplation that occurs in adoration, attentiveness, contemplation, and opening ourselves to receive God's grace. Active prayer is intercessory. It means to follow in the work of Christ, to work for the loving redemption of the world, to let our hands and feet be those of Jesus. After all, Evelyn reminded us, "redemption does not mean you and me made safe and popped into heaven. It means that each soul . . . is taken and used again for the spread of [Christ's] redeeming work."

Prayer shapes us for the work of love. Both prayer and love are necessary to get through our days with the anxieties, busyness, and sometimes suffering that occurs. Evelyn noted wryly that, "The bread of life seldom has any butter on it."

"[Most people] go through a correct [prayer] routine," Evelyn wrote, "learning from a book, but end up quite dry." Instead, Evelyn invited Christians to approach prayer in the manner described by Saint Catherine: try diving into the Great Pacific Ocean of God. "Real prayer," said Evelyn, "begins with a plunge into the water. Our movements may be quite incorrect, but they will be real."

Teach me Lord to be unafraid of the kind of "real prayer" Evelyn invites me to. Help me jump into the saving ocean of Your grace to wash away the hard barriers of individuality and embrace the abundant life You offer. Amen.

Aimee Semple McPherson

1890–1944

—

Spreading the Good News

It is not the great knowledge you have or how
important you are, but your willingness to let God fill
your life.

Aimee Semple McPherson, a notorious and charismatic figure
during the evangelical ferment of the early twentieth century,
believed that everyone has a sacred gift they should share with
the world. "It doesn't matter how rich one dies or how poor," she
insisted, "What matters is what you give while you're here." Having
put all that she had "on the altar for the Lord," she called others
to join her. Her preaching became so substantial and electrifying
that her followers coalesced into a new denomination, the Four-
square Gospel.

She spread the good news as a traveling preacher with her
mother and young children. Believed to be the first women to cross
the country alone in an automobile, Aimee traveled in a Packard
flanked with religious slogans on either door. She went from town
to town, preaching from her "Gospel Car," making converts and
performing faith healings. Soon, she gathered a loyal following and
attracted attention from the media. And eventually, she and her

family settled in Los Angeles where she raised enough money to build the denomination's headquarters, the Angelus Temple, which was large enough to seat over five thousand.

A consummate publicist and performer, Aimee's charisma brought her and the church many devotees. But she was often criticized for her dramatic flair, and drew further controversy when she mysteriously disappeared while swimming in the ocean one day. Weeks later, she reappeared, claiming she had been kidnapped. And although many of her followers believed her, skeptics considered it a hoax to cover up clandestine trysts with her lover.

Despite her unorthodox behavior, Aimee's desire to spread God's love to all people was unequivocal. And her conviction that she could do so was insurmountable. She once declared, "With God, I can do all things! With God in you, and the people whom you can interest, by the grace of God, we're going to cover the world!"

With her simple call to participate in the good news, Aimee stirred countless people to faith. She believed that this privilege and responsibility belonged to everyone. Her duty was to channel her charisma to spread God's love. And in fulfilling her call, she asks us to do the same: to share that singular gift we possess to help others to God. She proclaimed, "We can all do our best, no matter how little it may be. This is my task and it is your task. I am your sister and you are my sister and brother in Christ. In God's name, let us get together."

> *God of my life, You call me to Your work in all of my imperfections. Help me see that I can act on my life's purpose even when you have not finished with me yet. Amen.*

Dorothy Day

1897–1980

⌒

A Revolution of the Heart

I believe some people—lots of people—pray to the witness of their lives through the work they do, the friendships they have, the love they offer people and receive from people. Since when are words the only acceptable form of prayer?

As Dorothy Day saw it, our actions forge our character. Words matter, but the Spirit is revealed through what we do, not just what we say or think. Her standards were high. If we profess to be Christian, our life should show it.

The only way she knew to sustain a life modeled on Christ was to build it on the Benedictine principle of *ora et labora,* prayer and work. Embodying the principle of prayer in action, Dorothy's prayer life was the bedrock upon which she built considerable achievements. Her life eloquently illustrates how our prayers can be transformed into writing, community, conversation, and everyday acts of mercy.

Dorothy was not always so pious, however. Throughout her childhood, teenage years, and twenties, she rarely crossed the threshold of a church. Eventually she found herself drawn toward the Catholic principles of embracing the poor. After meeting and listening to the "Easy Essays" of Peter Maurin, a former Catholic brother and holy hobo from France, they found a way to revolutionize society and create the conditions of the kingdom right here on earth, among and with the most marginalized of people.

The two sat at Dorothy's kitchen table and wrote the first articles for a new publication, the *Catholic Worker*. It sold for only a penny a copy, which is the price it is still available for today. People snapped it up. Eagerly they began to read about nonviolence, economic and racial justice, and the certainty of Christ's loving forgiveness. Soon readers were knocking on her door, asking how they could help her or be helped by her. This paper, written at Dorothy's kitchen table, gave birth to a movement.

From its beginning, the Catholic Worker movement grew into a network of houses of hospitality where people who were hungry, homeless, or broken, could find refuge from the pressures of an uncaring society. Christian love was more than an idea between the walls of these houses. All people—regardless of their circumstances or how they looked—were treated with the God-given dignity due to every human being. *When a social worker asked Dorothy how long her "clients" were "allowed" to stay in the hospitality house, she answered,* "We let them stay forever. They live with us, they die with us, and we give them a Christian burial. We pray for them after they are dead. Once they are taken in, they become members of the family. Or rather, they always were members of the family. They are our brothers and sisters in Christ."

Today more than 150 Catholic Worker communities still serve in the darkness, lighting the way of hospitality to the homeless, hungry, and exiled. As Dorothy said, *"The greatest challenge of the day is: how to bring about a revolution of the heart, a revolution which has to start with each one of us."* Such theology is created from the inside out. As Dorothy well knew, our actions make visible the hidden revolutions of the heart.

May the prayer for Dorothy's canonization become our
prayer: "Merciful God, you called your servant Dorothy
Day to show us the face of Jesus in the poor and
forsaken. By constant practice of the works of mercy, she
embraced poverty and witnessed steadfastly to justice
and peace." May I be inspired by her to become my
best self. Amen.

Radical Love

The mystery of the poor is this: That they are Jesus, and
what you do for them you do for Him. It is the only
way we have of knowing and believing in our love.

Dorothy Day's life shattered again and again. Her history included early sexual affairs, an abortion, separation from the father
of her daughter, and raising her child alone. She knew what it
was like to live poor and to feel lonely. Her gift was that she was
able to start with the messiness of her own life to get closer and
closer to Jesus.

In the beginning, Dorothy was drawn to radical justice, but
in a political rather than a religious way. She was a self-avowed
anarchist who went to jail for protesting that women should have
the right to vote. She abhorred unequal wealth and considered
America's de facto class system one of the evils of capitalism. Her
friends were shocked, then, when she began to attend the Catholic
Church in her neighborhood.

At the expense of dear friendships, Dorothy felt called to the
radical love of Jesus more than the radical politics of her comrades. She described her life as "a succession of events that led

me to Jesus' feet, glimpses of Him that I received through many years which made me feel the vital need of Him and of religion." And she was never in any doubt about what it meant to love your neighbor. "The Corporal Works are to feed the hungry, to give drink to the thirsty, to clothe the naked, to ransom the captive, to harbor the harborless, to visit the sick, and to bury the dead." These were more than nice words in the Baltimore Catechism; they were Christ's direction for living a worthwhile life.

When loving became difficult, as it did time and again, Dorothy fortified herself with the assurance that suffering was also basic to her religious call. "During the summer when things were going hard, I grimly modified grace before meals: 'We give Thee thanks, O Lord, for these Thy gifts, and for all our tribulations, from Thy bounty, through Christ our Lord, Amen.'" She believed that it was a privilege to share in the suffering of her Lord.

Even before her death, Dorothy was regarded by many as a living saint. Never mind her famous reply, "Don't call me a saint. I don't want to be dismissed so easily." She wanted people to understand that loving was hard work. She found strange reassurance in Dostoyevsky's reminder that love in action is a "harsh and dreadful thing compared to love in dreams." It had more to do with being responsive to the unique individuality of each person than with any dogma. It might be easy to talk about love, but to really love others, day after day, requires a connection to the living waters of divine energy and a healthy measure of stamina.

> *I pray to you, good Jesus, as Dorothy prayed: that I might love radically, as is Your way. You ask me to stand with the poor and forgotten. May I have the strength to do so when the tribulations come, remembering Your suffering became the path to God's promise. Amen.*

Our Common Humanity

I always felt the common unity of our humanity; the longing of the human heart is for this communion.

Dorothy Day had an instinct for the authentic. She saw through the empty forms and fancy words of people who did and said the right things but had no connection to the power of Christ's message. "The longer I live," she wrote, "the more I see God at work in people who don't have the slightest interest in religion and never read the Bible and wouldn't know what to do if they were persuaded to go inside a church."

For Dorothy, there was a direct connection between the bread broken at Communion and the bread shared at shelters and soup kitchens. One gave meaning to the other. Church is what happens when people relate to each other in love. Christ is present in the liturgy and present when one person listens with compassion to the pain of another.

Dorothy was wary of those who came to the Catholic Worker hospitality houses to sightsee. She didn't think that watching, observing, or analyzing others brought people into compassionate relationships: "You should not write the things you do unless you mean them. In other words, do not write about hospitality unless you are willing to assume the obligations such writing brings with it." She was engaged in a relationship with Christ through the people who happened to be in front of her. And she recoiled at the suggestion that she was Lady Bountiful, handing out packages of goodness to those less fortunate. She was not a superior giving to the needy. "I felt that charity was a word to choke over. Who wanted charity?" She knew that what people wanted was the same thing she wanted—to be part of the community of all human beings, be they rich or poor, favored or ill-favored.

God of compassion, You are in all things—the beautiful, the ugly, the joyful, and the painful. Sharpen my vision so that I may see past the cloudiness of my own eyes to the authentic community You offer me. Amen.

Gertrude Behanna

1900–1976

Definitely for God

Is this for God, or is this for Gert?
If it's for God, we try to do it;
if it's for Gert, we try not to do it.
If we don't know, we wait.

A selfish, cynical alcoholic, Gertrude Behanna used drugs, and had attempted suicide. Nothing in her life was working. Though she was raised in a family that surrounded her with all the material wealth she could want, her soul was impoverished. It was the night she was invited to have dinner with a Christian couple, of all things, that changed her life.

Making no attempt to curb her usual obnoxious behavior, Gert drank too much and used her messy life story to try and shock the couple. After listening quietly, the man finally suggested, "Why don't you turn your troubles over to God?"

Stupefied, Gert recalled later: "It stopped me! . . . There sat this sophisticated New York businessman actually believing that there was Someone to whom I could turn over my problems. I looked at him, and said, 'You make it sound as though I had suitcases too heavy to carry, and I needed a porter.' He said, 'That's about it.'"

Gert's dinner companions followed up by mailing a note and magazine. "This amazed me," she wrote. "They had only seen me one evening, and I had been a total mess. Why did they care? This was my initial introduction to the courtesy of Christ." The couple wrote that they would pray for her. "This rocked me. Pray for me! So far as I know, no one in my whole life had ever prayed for me. And God knows I'd never prayed for anyone."

Opening the magazine, Gert read the article "It Is Never Too Late to Start Over," and "did something I'd never done in my life before; I went over to my bed and got down on my knees. In about 20 minutes, it was all over. Of course there are no words. All I know is that it was more like a spiritual shower-bath than anything. I felt cleansed. I also felt welcomed. I also felt forgiven."

In that moment, Gert's self-centeredness was transformed into a desire to serve others. Over the next few months, she gave away most of her wealth and welcomed women who had nowhere else to go into her modest home. When others praised her selfless acts, Gert responded: "I am nothing in the world but a cracked, chipped, rusty old pipeline! It just shows what 'odds and ends' Christ can use."

Gert spent the remainder of her life "trying to find out what Love is—how to live it, and how to give it away!" For her, this meant noticing and trying to eliminate the judgments she made about others. "Once I began to recover, I no longer looked down on people; but then I had the final battle that I had to fight, and that was looking down on people who looked down on people." In the end, Gertrude Behanna had found love.

> *God, help me to find those places where I still sit in judgment and let Gert be my model as I learn how to live love and how to love others. Amen.*

Anne Morrow Lindbergh

1906–2001

Ebb and Flow of Life

The problem . . . is more basically: how to remain whole in the midst of the distractions of life; how to remain balanced, no matter what centrifugal forces tend to pull one off center; how to remain strong, no matter what shocks come in at the periphery and tend to crack the hub of the wheel.

No wonder Anne Morrow Lindbergh wrote about the struggles of daily life! Wife of aviation pioneer Charles Lindbergh and flight pioneer in her own right, she chronicled her early years defying gravity in two books, *North to the Orient* and *Listen! The Wind.* Mother of six, her oldest was kidnapped and murdered in one of the most publicized crimes of the twentieth century. Familiar with an extremely full emotional range—from chaos and grief to joy and accomplishment—Anne understood what it means to be a woman struggling with family and career. In midlife, this struggle birthed her book *Gift from the Sea.*

Considering seashells as metaphors of the challenges women face, each shell mirrored back to Anne an intrinsic piece of the cosmological whole that is a well lived, balanced life. In the shell's channeled whelk, she saw the occasional need to pare down to essentials, reducing the complexities of modern family life to its simplest essence. The need for solitude was reflected in the moon shell. "Only when one is connected to one's core, is one connected to others."

Drinking deep from this secluded wellspring, Anne came to realize that being of service to others in a pure and deliberate way created a "giving that seems to renew itself even in the act of depletion." In the double-sunrise shell, she contemplated the intensely exclusive quality inherent in the early stages of adult partnership and the mother–child bond. Feeling their transience, she wrote "One learns to accept the fact that no permanent return is possible to an old form of relationship; and, more deeply still, that there is no holding of a relationship to a single form. This is not a tragedy but part of the ever recurrent miracle of life and growth."

On the beach, Anne found the cycles of a woman's life. In the oyster bed, she contemplated family life and saw the sea creature "fitted and formed by its own life and struggle to survive . . . untidy, spread out in all directions, heavily encrusted with accumulations and, in its living state, firmly embedded on its rock." And finally, in the argonaut, Anne imagined time beyond the oyster bed, time when "we are adventuring in the chartless seas of imagination."

An insightful and valiant woman whose grief and triumph were painfully public, Anne Morrow Lindbergh's wisdom—gleaned from her time spent with the rise and fall of the salt water tides—endures in her little book. Since the 1950s, her quiet musings on shells have guided and accompanied others on their inner journey. In the end, she leaves each reader/journeyer with "perhaps the most important thing for me to take back from beach living: simply the memory that each cycle of the tide is valid; each cycle of the wave is valid; each cycle of relationship is valid."

> *God, Creator of the sea and its seemingly empty shells,*
> *enable me to see simplicity in complexity, wisdom and*
> *wonder in the everyday, and the eternal value of life's*
> *ebb and flow. Amen.*

Peace Pilgrim

1908–1981

—

Striding Toward Peace

[I shall] remain a wanderer until mankind has learned the way of peace.

At the age of forty-five, Mildred Norman Ryder literally walked the length and breadth of the North American continent with nothing save her tenacious faith in God's love to provide for her. And not just once. Over the course of twenty-eight years, she crossed the continent seven times. The implicit prayer in her every step was this: "overcome evil with good, falsehood with truth, and hatred with love." The embodiment of Mildred's faith resulted in a serenity that earned her national recognition by the name she adopted: Peace Pilgrim.

Peace Pilgrim's journey began with a sacred restlessness. A melancholy had descended on her that made her feel less and less at peace within herself. An unhappy marriage intensified her despair. Finally, one night in 1938, depression overwhelmed her. She knew nothing else to do but to let her restlessness lead her. She walked through the woods all night, beseeching God to illuminate her path in life, praying, "Please use me! Here I am—take all of me and use me as you will. I withhold nothing." Alone in that forest, Mildred had a spiritual experience that forever changed her and convinced her that "there is guidance that comes from within to all who will listen."

The answer to her prayer began slowly changing her life. She felt compelled to pare down her cluttered life to only what was most essential and slowly gave away all her possessions. In 1953, at the height of the McCarthy Era and during the Korean War, she had a vision that designated her a pilgrim, destined to walk for peace. By then, her only personal belongings were a comb, a toothbrush, and a pen. She had no plan, no itinerary, and no logistical support. Her mission was simply to "walk according to the highest light we have, encountering lovingly those who are out of harmony."

On her pilgrimage, Mildred never approached anyone, never proselytized. She waited for people to approach her. She became a living, walking prayer. And in all her journeys, this Peace Pilgrim was never threatened or harmed. She experienced that "no one walks so safely as one who walks with great love and great faith." She became the message of peace she wished most to give to the world.

Just as she touched thousands of lives during a time of war and distrust, she appeals to us still: "One little person, giving all of her time to peace, makes news. Many people, giving some of their time, can make history."

> *Dear God, walking in peace is an act of power.*
> *May I join in Peace Pilgrim's footsteps.*
> *May my path be my testimony to You. Amen.*

Simone Weil

1909–1943

The Red Virgin

I had never foreseen the possibility . . . of a real
contact, person to person, here below, between a human
being and God.

Simone Weil was born in Paris in 1909—a time when it was
unacceptable for a woman to be a philosopher. And yet today she
is known as one of the most challenging thinkers of the twentieth
century. She is revered most, however, for her mystical experience
of God's love. Although her political essays and articles published
during her life labeled her a Socialist activist, the notebooks and
letters published after her death led to her recognition, in the
words of as T. S. Eliot, as "a woman of genius, of a kind of genius,
akin to that of the saints."

After graduating from the École Normale Superieure in 1931,
Simone began teaching. Indignant over the injustices of the poor,
she protested alongside factory workers. Eventually, she left teaching to work as a laborer in a Renault factory to experience the
hardships of the working class. In 1936, she traveled to Barcelona
to share in the sufferings of the Republican Army during the Spanish Civil War. To her comrades, Simone seemed to be anarchist and
part nun—earning her an affectionate nickname: the Red Virgin.

And yet, alongside this activism and social engagement, there was a different story. In 1937, Simone visited the chapel of Santa Maria degli Angeli, the same chapel in which St Francis of Assisi often prayed. Simone recorded the flood of emotion: "Something stronger than I compelled me for the first time in my life to go down on my knees." The encounter was of "a presence more personal, more certain, and more real than that of a human being."

Simone was raised agnostic in a secular Jewish home, and she declared herself to be outside of any religious tradition. Still, she experienced the reality of God. She instructs that once we move past our intellectual conceptions of God, "we end by touching something that is the central essence, necessary and pure, something not of the senses, common to joy and sorrow: the very love of God."

Her peer, Simone de Beauvoir, recorded this memory of Simone: "A great famine had broken out in China, and I was told that when she heard the news, she had wept. These tears compelled my respect, much more than her gifts as a philosopher. I envied her having a heart that could beat across the world." This is the love that called Simone to social justice work. Simone's life demonstrates that the wisdom of God is found not in the intellect but in the actions of the heart.

> *God, guide me past my thoughts of you to the experience of Your presence. Strengthen my heart, so that I, like Simone, can embrace the truth You have for me. Amen.*

Rosa Louise Parks

1913–2006

—

Standing in Your Truth

I was there. I took that stand.

It was cold that day in December 1955 when Rosa Parks got on a bus in Montgomery, Alabama. She was tired, but no more so than usual after a day working as a seamstress. She made her way to the back of the bus and sat down in the "colored section," as she had hundreds of times before. But this time, when the bus driver came toward her and asked her to give up her seat to a white man, she refused. She would have gotten up for an elderly person or a child, but she would not stand just so an able-bodied white man could take her seat. "People always say that I didn't get up because I was tired," she later said, "but that isn't true. I was not tired physically. . . . No, the only tired I was, was tired of giving in."

Her seemingly simple act of refusal eventually changed the law of the land. Rosa's arrest and trial became the center of a nationwide protest, culminating in the 381-day bus boycott in Montgomery. She was convicted and fined. But she refused to pay the fine, and her lawyers appealed the case. Eventually, the US Supreme Court ruled in November 1956 that racial segregation on all forms of public transportation was unconstitutional.

Rosa's act of defiance was a spontaneous act of courage. But it was also a moment she was prepared for. Although she was a job-holding, church-going, law-abiding family member, she was also politically active. She had been a member of Montgomery's chapter of the NAACP since 1943 and was a member of the Women's Political Council. She knew about nonviolent civil disobedience.

Rosa's childhood also prepared her to be courageous. She grew up attending the African Methodist Episcopal Church and hearing her grandmother reading from the Bible and grandfather offering prayers. As a young girl, she learned to steady her courage when the KKK rode by her house at night. She would go to sleep, curled up beside her grandfather, and next to the loaded shotgun he used for defense.

She made it a point to read the Bible every day. "I remember finding such comfort and peace while reading the Bible. Its teaching became a way of life and helped me in dealing with my day-to-day problems." Rosa also learned that the Bible told a sacred history of people trying to do what was right. "From my upbringing and the Bible, I learned people should stand up for rights, just as the children of Israel stood up to the Pharaoh." Although "standing up" for Rosa meant staying seated, she knew what she had to do when she met the Pharaoh on that bus in Alabama.

In dark moments, Rosa relied on Psalm 27 for courage: "The Lord is my light and my salvation; whom shall I fear? The Lord is the strength of my life; of whom shall I be afraid?" Amen.

Etty Hillesum

1914–1943

~

One Great Meaningful Whole

There among the barracks, full of hunted and persecuted people, I found confirmation of my love of life. Not for one moment was I cut off from the life I was said to have left behind. There was simply one, great, meaningful whole.

Etty Hillesum writes about the seemingly impossible subject of how love filled and surrounded her in the Nazi concentration camps of World War II. This Jewish woman found life and meaning in the suffering of the camps. She found God in the camps. Reading her diaries is like watching a mystical transformation occurring in the midst of evil. Over time, Etty developed an understanding of how God is present in the most heart-breaking situations.

Her journey began when her country, Holland, was overtaken by the Nazi occupation. Shocked by the brutality of the Nazis, Etty wrote, "It is sometimes hard to take in and comprehend, oh God, what those created in Your likeness do to each other in these disjointed days. I no longer shut myself away in my room, God, I try to look things straight in the face, even the worst crimes."

During the early months of the occupation, Etty was given permission to travel from Amsterdam to the transport camp at Westerbork to volunteer in the hospital there. To capture her thoughts and deal with her experiences, she began to write letters and diaries that weren't discovered until 1981. Her writings have since become an invaluable document of the Jewish experience during the war. More than that, they are a record of what is best in the human spirit: the light that can shine through, even in the most challenging time and place.

A lot of what she wrestles with in her writings has to do with whether love can exist in a world that is the embodiment of hatred: "Many feel that their love of mankind languishes at Westerbork because . . . people here don't give you much occasion to love them. But I keep discovering that there is no direct connection between people's behavior and the love you feel for them. Love for one's fellow man is like an elemental glow that sustains you." She discovered, even dying in a concentration camp, a wellspring of love inside of her, the source of which was God.

Etty came to believe that answering hate with hate made no sense. "Every atom of hate we add to this world makes it still more inhospitable." And she came to understand how false it was to think that those people are bad, but we are good. Her experiences showed her otherwise: we all have the capacity for selfish, grim behavior. "The rottenness of others is in us too." She insisted, "I no longer believe that we can change anything in the world until we have first changed ourselves. And that seems to me the only lesson to be learned from this war. That we must look into ourselves and nowhere else."

She was able to move her ideas from her head to her heart and feel love and forgiveness for the tormentors. "I knew at once: I shall have to pray for this German soldier. Out of all those uniforms, one has been given a face now. There will be other faces, too, in which we shall have to read something we understand: that German soldiers suffer as well. There are no frontiers between suffering people, and we must pray for them all."

Etty died in Auschwitz on November 30, 1943. One of her last entries was, "God, I am grateful for everything. I shall live on with that part of the dead that lives forever."

God, I am moved by Etty's life. Let the wellspring inside me, and fed by my faith in You, transform the irritation and hatred I feel for others into an abiding love for all humanity. Amen.

―

Inner Freedom

How is it that this stretch of heathland surrounded by barbed wire, through which so much human misery has flooded, nevertheless remains inscribed in my memory as something almost lovely?

Before she died at Auschwitz, Etty Hillesum was given the gift of understanding something profound about the reality of God's love. You can be free, and you can be loved in any and every situation life presents. Nothing and no one can take away your inner freedom, including death. Her experiences as a Jew during the Nazi occupation served to teach her these truths. Of being in the camp, she wrote, "Our ultimate human values are being put to the test. Life's innermost framework is stripped of all outer trappings."

Early passages from her diary show Etty discovering how to go on living as despair gathered around her: "I draw prayer round me like a dark, protective wall, withdraw inside it as one might into a convent cell and then step outside again, calmer and stronger and more collected." Increasingly, she was able to hold inside her two, opposing realities at the same time. She saw the atrocities, and at the same time, experienced a mystical union with the divine that allowed her to see the aching beauty of life.

> I thought, how strange. It is wartime. There are concentration camps. I can say of so many of the houses I pass: here the son has been thrown into prison, there the father has been taken hostage, and an eighteen-year-old boy in that house over there has been sentenced to death. I know about the mounting human suffering. I know the persecution and oppression and despotism and the impotent fury and terrible sadism. I know it all.
>
> And yet—at unguarded moments, when left to myself, I suddenly lie against the naked breast of life, and her arms round me are so gentle and so protective.

Etty came to the conclusion that "if you have a rich inner life, there probably isn't all that much difference between the inside and outside of a camp." She used the terrible things she witnessed to test her ideas about the power of the inner life, and ultimately found that the indwelling of God's love could withstand the horror of the camp. She concluded that "We carry everything within us, God and Heaven and Hell and Earth and Life and Death and all of history. The externals are simply so many props; everything we need is within us." Her experience kept confirming her conviction that inner freedom was always hers, no matter what. "I do not feel I have been robbed of my freedom; essentially, no one can do me any harm at all."

On September 7, 1943, Etty boarded a train for Auschwitz. As the train pulled away, she threw a postcard out the window. On it, she wrote: "We left the camp singing." She was twenty-nine years old.

*God of freedom, I pray for even some of the strength
that Etty had. May I always remember that nothing
can really harm me. You are all I need. In You, I am
free. In You, I am loved. Nothing can ever kill my
spirit. Amen.*

Fannie Lou Hamer

1917–1977

Revolutionary Faith

Christ was a revolutionary person, out there where it
was happening. That's what God is all about, and that's
where I get my strength.

Fannie Lou Hamer is a national symbol of the participation
of poor southern blacks in the civil rights movement. Born the
twentieth child to Mississippi sharecroppers, Fannie Lou started
picking and baling cotton at the age of six. She dropped out of
school at twelve to help support her family.

In 1962, workers from the Student Nonviolent Coordinating
Committee (SNCC) visited her church, encouraging blacks to
register to vote. "I didn't know anything about registering to vote,"
she recalled. "They were talking about we could vote out people
that we didn't want in office. That sounded interesting enough to
me that I wanted to try it."

"Trying it" was easier said than done. Fannie Lou went with
seventeen other blacks to register. At the circuit clerk's office, they
were confronted with men holding rifles. When she got home,
the owner of the land she'd lived on for eighteen years told her
that he didn't need her help to register: "I answered the only way
I could and told him that I didn't go down there to register for
him; I went down there to register for myself." He immediately
told her to leave his farm.

Fannie Lou joined SNCC as a fieldworker in voter registration drives and later helped organize the Mississippi Freedom Democratic Party. "I guess if I'd had any sense, I'd have been scared—but what was the point of being scared? The only thing [white people] could do was kill me, and it seemed they'd been trying to do that a little at a time since I could remember," she quipped.

Jailed with other civil rights workers in 1963, Fannie Lou was so severely beaten that she suffered permanent kidney damage and was blinded in one eye. When people asked her why she persevered, she replied, "Whether I want to do it or not, I got to. This is my calling. This is my mission." She was known for singing hymns in the midst of her protests. Her favorites included "This Little Light of Mine" and "Let Your Light So Shine." She would beam, "It brings out the soul."

As a member of the Mississippi Freedom Democratic Party, Fannie Lou traveled to the National Democratic Convention in 1964 to protest the all-white state delegation. She gave a moving address. Her story was aired on national television later that evening: "I found out after that women and men from all over the country wept when I was testifying—because when I testified, I was crying too." In response to the overwhelming outrage, Democrats agreed that in the future no delegation would be seated from a state where anyone was illegally denied the vote.

Fannie Lou dedicated her life so that all could have an equal say in the running of their country.

> *God of all, your fire ignites the old as well as the young.*
> *I know it's never too late to start changing the world.*
> *May I remember Fannie Lou as a beacon. Amen.*

Madeleine L'Engle

1918–2007

———

The Call of the Artist

*Artistic temperament . . . sometimes seems a
battleground, a dark angel of destruction and a bright
angel of creativity wrestling.*

Madeleine L'Engle knew that obeying the call of the artist can
be agonizing. It is painful to wrestle with your experience and birth
your truth. Madeleine published over sixty books, so it might look
as if her ride was easy. But that was not true. She wrote honestly
about the difficulties she had being obedient to her God-given
passion for writing.

In her best-known work, *A Wrinkle in Time*, she explored the
strange world of quantum physics and the nature of relationships
in the universe. God erupts into the action in the most unexpected
ways. Her books cast a large net, reaching beyond Christian and
young audiences into the imagination of anyone who likes a
good story told with adventure. She saw that the "chief difference
between the Christian and the secular artist is the purpose of the
work, which is to further the coming of the Kingdom, and to turn
our feet toward home." This purpose runs through all her work,
whether poetry, fiction, or nonfiction.

As a young mother, Madeleine was so busy with family and running her family's general store that her life became "the perfect 'way
not' to write a book." She grew so discouraged at one point that

she tried to give up writing altogether. But she couldn't shake her calling. She finally surrendered to her God-given talent when she found herself outlining a book about the failure to write a book. She concluded, "If we're given a talent, you have to serve it. You don't own it. You don't control it. You don't manipulate it. You can do that and be a best-seller if you want to. But ultimately it is a gift that is freely given and you have to serve your gift."

It took ten years for *A Wrinkle in Time* to find a publisher. But when the book finally came out, it sold over six million copies and won the Newbery Medal. In subsequent years, her advice, was simple: "Do what you think you ought to do," she said, "even if it's nontraditional." In retrospect, Madeleine understood how essential it is to surrender to the creative urge. She became even more certain that on the deepest level, we are given a gift from God that is ours to bring forth: "To paint a picture or to write a story or to compose a song is an incarnational activity. In a very real sense, the artist should be like Mary who, when the angel told her that she was to bear the Messiah, was obedient."

But this obedience is anything but passive. To serve one's gift requires daily recommitment to the practice of your skill. And it requires an alertness to the moment when something universal speaks through your gift: "Unless a writer works constantly to improve and refine the tools of his trade they will be useless instruments if and when the moment of inspiration, of revelation, does come. This is the moment when a writer is spoken through, the moment that a writer must accept with gratitude and humility, and then attempt, as best he can, to communicate to others."

God of the universe, may I be true to my calling. May I remember Madeleine's story and that creativity is incarnational, and that I alone can bring to light my part of the truth. Amen.

Evelina Lopez Antonetty

1922–1984

The Mother of the South Bronx

We will never stop struggling here in the Bronx, even though they have destroyed it around us. We would rather pitch tents . . . than move from here. We would fight back. There is nothing that we would not do.

Start any conversation about schools, children, and Puerto Ricans in New York City, and the name Evelina Lopez Antonetty is uttered in complete reverence. She was direct and tough. New York City Mayors John Lindsay and Ed Koch both took her calls.

Immigrating to New York City in the midst of the Great Depression, eleven-year-old Evelina made the trip alone, speaking no English. True to the fearless energy she exhibited throughout her life, Evelina found opportunities for service everywhere. Sustained by "a wonderful family that believed in the power of God, Spirit, and industry," she rolled up her sleeves and set about making her small corner of the city a better place to live.

She learned English quickly, and used her newfound voice to help her Puerto Rican neighbors. Many were starving because they didn't know English well enough to fill out forms for financial aid. So, Evelina got a stack of forms and, translating for her neighbors, filled in their answers, submitted the forms, and hauled bags of groceries to hungry families.

Marrying and having children only intensified Evelina's dedication to grassroots reform. Appalled at the lack of responsiveness public schools had toward minority children, she created United Bronx Parents, a grassroots, voluntary advocacy organization. Under her spirited leadership, United Bronx Parents lobbied for bilingual teachers, parent education, greater teacher accountability, and more community influence in schools. Alliances were created with other minority communities, and Evelina's crowning achievement was the establishment of standardized education within New York City.

"They will never take us away from here," said the woman whose life is a legacy of positive action in the South Bronx. "I feel very much a part of this place and I am never going to leave. And, after me, my children will be here to carry on . . . I have very strong children . . . and very strong grandchildren." Due to Evelina's spirit, not only her own children and grandchildren enjoy proper educations in New York City, but every child in the city is better off for her tireless efforts.

God of righteousness, make me Your voice. Make me Your word. Make me the pure energy of Your reforming spirit. Amen.

Letty Russell

1926–2007

—

Talking Back

Instead of worrying that we will lose our faith as feminists, we should be celebrating the fact that we have been given gifts that will allow us to talk back to tradition.

Letty Russell spent her whole adult life "trying to figure out how to subvert the church into being the church." As one of the foremothers of feminist liberation theology, Letty was known for her uncanny ability to juggle a prophetic critique of Christianity from within its sacred tradition.

When Letty told her father she wanted to be a minister, he was direct in his reply. "He said that as a minister, I'd always be a misfit; it was fine if I wanted to do it, but I'd never make any money." She laughed and added, "He was a businessman." In the 1950s, Letty was one of the first women admitted to Harvard Divinity School and one of the first women to be ordained by the Presbyterian Church. She got her first job at an innovative, multiracial church in East Harlem where the pastors, men and women, lived and worked together for civil rights. "In that context I had no trouble being a leader," said Letty. "It was a very open place to work, because there was so much to do and there was so much breakdown in society that normal gender roles weren't enforced." She served as a working pastor for nearly twenty years.

Her experience of applied theology in East Harlem led her into other liberation movements, always seeking to understand "the meaning of God's action in situations of oppression." As a professor of feminist theology at Yale Divinity School where she went after her pastoral work, Letty took on topics that other teachers avoided—feminist hermeneutics, gay and lesbian theology, Third World theology, and racism. She required her students to learn how to "think from the other end," a methodology that takes the point of view of the other, the less advantaged.

Every so often someone would suggest that it might make sense for women to leave a church with its two-thousand-year-old tradition of patriarchy. But Letty disagreed: "It is impossible for me and for many other alienated women and men to walk away from the church, for it has been the bearer of the story of Jesus Christ and the good news of God's love. It seems rather that we have to sit back and ask ourselves about what is happening among us when two or three gather in Christ's name and begin to think through possible ways of being church that will affirm the full humanity of all women and men."

Letty encouraged all who care about justice to become more skilled in the art of "thinking from the other end," from the point of view of the other. She promoted "talking back," engaging directly when we have questions or our experience differs from what's presented as the norm. Letty believed that through our questions, we become more faithful to God's call for us. We are not called to be timid. We are called to use all our gifts in their full measure.

> *God, it is only natural that when we see injustice around us, we are disturbed. Give us the courage to talk back in a way that illuminates hypocrisy and brings greater unity within your church. Give us discernment and courage. Amen.*

Mending Creation

When we come together to celebrate at God's welcome table with our sister and brother outsiders, part of our kitchen table spirituality will be that of worrying with God.

Patriarchal systems categorize and separate. While these functions can be useful, if left unchecked they can "divide our social body, each one living by domination of one over the other." By contrast, ecofeminism emphasizes our connectivity. We are all one sacred body, Letty affirmed, and it is ultimately each person's task to help keep this body mended and whole.

For Letty, the norm of Christian theology did not lie in the past, but in how we look toward and prepare for the future. And ecofeminism is a key aspect of this preparation. "A positive word born of two negative situations, the destruction of the natural world and the oppression of women," ecofeminism makes the connection between the struggle for women's worth and respect for all of nature. Women's voices are still not at full capacity. The integrity of nature is being compromised and destroyed. And in Letty's view, it falls upon each one of us to "mend the creation"—that is, to establish new relationships of mutuality involving an inner transformation of mind, spirit, and worldviews. We can learn from the interconnectivity of the whole of creation, and the wisdom gleaned here will help us transform not only our relationship to the earth but unjust social structures as well.

Letty offered three clues to live into what she called "God's future." First, we need to live with questions rather than answers.

"In a changing world, there are only changing answers." Second, we need eyes of faith to enable us to see the world from God's perspective. And third, we need to celebrate life, all of life, and the world in which we live. May we, as Letty did, enjoy the world in which we live, "simply because it is God's world!"

> *Oh God, I hear the pains and groans of creation*
> *neglected and abused. Give me the consciousness to*
> *know how to help with the mending of Your glorious*
> *creation. Amen.*

A Table of Peace

The Bible presents a story of God's love affair with the world, a vision of New Creation.

Letty Russell helped a whole generation of women recast themselves in the center of Christ's vision of what she called "God's New Creation." She crafted theological arguments based on a biblical vision she felt must be interpreted anew by each generation. Yet she discussed how difficult it can be for women to look to these texts for support. She was convinced that, if we are seriously engaged in understanding God's New Creation, we will find "the dangerous memory of the future" in the scriptures.

Counseling us not to take the words literally, Letty urged us instead to constantly test the text's meaning against our own intellectual understanding as well as that of the community. We must talk to each other while we quilted a new theology from the bits and pieces of our religious traditions. By doing this, we could "piece together the message of God's love in a way that is seriously imaginable as good news for them as well as for others."

Letty was also a catalyst for women who wanted to become theologians and ministers. She midwifed an International Feminist Doctorate of Ministry program, which was especially geared to the needs of Third World women.

At the end of each of her courses, Letty invited her students to her home to share a "shalom meal." Shalom is the Hebrew word for hello, goodbye, and peace. Jews around the world come together for these dinners. Always informal, and full of abundant food and drink, these gatherings are a time for laughter, storytelling, and singing. Peace is definitely what Letty's students encountered as they entered her warm and welcoming home. Soon they discovered that, in the midst of the celebrating, a "community" formed, and the seeds of lifelong friendships were sown. During this joyous meal, Letty reminded her students that what they were experiencing was a glimpse of God's gift of shalom to all creation, a preview of the New Creation that God, in Jesus Christ, has promised to all.

Over the years, Letty's shalom meals—shared around a round table where no one was excluded, and where those who had been historically marginalized held the seats of honor—become a powerful metaphor for God's liberating promise that stretches before all humanity.

> *God, your gift of shalom is available to all creation. Let us, like Letty, gather those who feel excluded from your embrace to gather at a round table and celebrate your liberating promise. Amen.*

Elizabeth O'Connor

1928–1998

—

The Sacred Art of Listening

The great task we have as Christians is to create communities where we can explore our discontent, our fears and self-doubt.

God emerges when we gather together as loving community. In community, we come face to face with the mystery of God's creation, with all its diversity and otherness. And although we all yearn for community, authentic connection is difficult for us to achieve. Elizabeth O'Conner instructs us to cultivate a form of listening that allows us to be open to the otherness of the other—a listening that fosters the sense of wonder in our relationships. It is this kind of listening that she suggests is both a sacred art as well as a spiritual practice.

Elizabeth came to Washington DC in 1952 with a plan to find a "healing environment for her Schizophrenic twin brother" (Menehan 1989:17). Intended as a short trip, a visit to The Church of the Savior resulted in her long tenure as writer, teacher, counselor and leader of small-groups in the church. Although she suffered from arthritis and other illnesses, Elizabeth lived a profound life that was ordinary, yet divinely inspiring. Her writings poignantly and beautifully gave voice to the journey and spirit of the early years of the church community.

Elizabeth taught people how to move into vital relationships with God and others. It takes dynamic listening. She asked the provocative question, "Are you listening to hear something that tallies with your own thoughts, or are you listening to find out?" "Listening to find out" is, in Elizabeth's view, truly an act of faith.

Most of us feel that others, and even God, need to conform to the way we see reality. After all, our egos reason, we *know* what is really going on. Elizabeth calls us into a radical not knowing. She suggests that we actively let go of our own expectations and allow our listening to be "alive, inquiring, curious, and therefore capable of discovery."

We live with the paradox that the more we go within to hear God, the more we reach a place of listening that connects us to others. Elizabeth suggests that through deep listening, "one touches a place of truth and freedom in one's self that is beyond the ordinary, a place where one is told the way to go." If only we have the ears to hear.

Elizabeth asserts we all have a purpose, and that purpose is to love. A community loves through listening for the sacred in our midst, which helps us remain open to the new that awaits us. It is a listening that fosters mutuality in communication, so that we can learn "to be radically obedient to the vision that has been given to us, saying, 'Here I am, send me.' God's Spirit descends on such a person."

> *O Loving God, during my encounter with others today,*
> *may Your spirit help me listen in a way that I am open*
> *to the wonder of others, the wonder of Your Creation.*
> *Amen.*

Maya Angelou

1928–2014

⌒

Inner Healing

I refuse utterly to use any of my energy in being bitter. Ever. I'll be angry, yes, but never that other thing. [It] is corrosive. It just kills you, gets you sick, makes you look old and ugly.

Maya Angelou's list of accomplishments would be impressive even for someone born into a life of privilege. Yet her early life couldn't have been more challenging.

At age three, she and her four-year-old brother traveled alone on a train to her grandmother's house in Arkansas. She was raped at eight. As a teenager, she gave birth to a son; unmarried, she completed high school the year after her son was born. Taking jobs where she could find them, she and her son lived paycheck to paycheck, never knowing if they'd have enough money each month for food or rent.

How was Maya able to survive and heal, given the challenges she faced as a child? For her, love is the healing balm that allows her to transcend bitterness:

> We, unaccustomed to courage
> exiles from delight
> live coiled in shells of loneliness

until love leaves its high holy temple
and comes into our sight
to liberate us into life.

Maya was liberated into life as a poet, playwright, editor, song-writer, singer, teacher, dancer, and civil rights activist. She was the first black woman to direct a television show, and the first black woman to have an original story scripted and made into a movie.

Her ability to overcome pain stems from Maya's unyielding conviction that she was not, nor had ever been, alone. "I am a firm believer that there is no place that God is not." Such a deep understanding offered her a strength that sustained her as she dove into pain. And it enabled her to rise again, not only unscathed but more alive for having taken the plunge:

> I keep on dying again.
> Veins collapse, opening like the
> Small fists of sleeping
> Children.
> Memory of old tombs,
> Rotting flesh and worms do
> Not convince me against
> The challenge. The years
> And cold defeat live deep in
> Lines along my face.
> They dull my eyes, yet
> I keep on dying,
> Because I love to live.

God, give me the courage to dive into my pain so that
I may transform my challenges into an inner healing
that can fuel my life with purpose and joy. Amen.

Real Christianity

*Many things continue to amaze me, even well into
the sixth decade of my life. I'm startled or taken aback
when people tell me they are Christians. My first
response is the question, "Already?"*

Growing up in the 1930s, Maya Angelou spent much of her
childhood with her grandmother in Stamps, Arkansas, a rural
town where segregation was so complete that many black children, according to Angelou, "didn't really, absolutely know what
whites looked like." Grandmother Henderson, called "Momma"
by Maya and her brother Bailey, marched the children to church
each Sunday, played host to visiting elders, and prayed and sang
hymns, often for the whole neighborhood to hear.

Maya would later become a best-selling author and worldwide
celebrity. Though she didn't often talk about her faith, when she
did, she made the point of saying, "It seems to me a lifelong en-
deavor to try to live the life of a Christian. I believe that is also true
for the Buddhist, for the Muslim, for the Jainist, for the Jew and
for the Taoist who try to live their beliefs. The idyllic condition
cannot be arrived at and held on to eternally. It is in the search
itself that one finds the ecstasy." And she often liked to paraphrase
the words of a colleague by offering this poem:

> When I say . . . "I am a Christian"
> I'm not shouting "I'm clean livin."
> I'm whispering "I was lost,
> Now I'm found and forgiven."

By penetrating the veneer of those who speak of faith, but whose lives shout otherwise, Maya invited us into a deeper integrity with ourselves and with the true spirit of God.

Peel back my veneer and falsehood, God, so all that remains to be seen is You and Your strength. Only through You will I find what is needed for my journey and I press toward that mark, with You as my guide. Amen.

Dorothee Soelle

1929–2003

The Role of Faith in Politics

The incomparable power of violence in our world today only deepens our yearning for true peace.

"How do we speak of God after Auschwitz?" This question knocked through Dorothee Soelle's mind over and over again. As a German political theologian, she was haunted by the Holocaust. Her primary philosophical concern focused on the meaning of the Nazi experience for Christians.

While she was studying literature at the University of Cologne in the late 1960s, Dorothee became part of a group of Christians who conducted monthly "political night prayer." This "prayer" consisted of reading about current events and analyzing them, followed by a scripture reading and a group reflection that drew the biblical texts together with the events. The evening concluded with a prayer and a discussion on practical action to be taken. This practice began to shape Dorothee's political theology.

As Dorothee continued to develop her theology in the 1980s, she would speak of herself as a German, a Protestant Christian, and a woman. As a German, the Holocaust not only challenged her country's soul, it also raised issues of the ongoing threats to life on earth from the postwar capitalistic economic order. For Dorothee, the threatened future holocaust of the entire planet must be the context for theology. And thus, as a Protestant Christian, she urged us to embrace mutual service and solidarity.

At first, Dorothee viewed feminism as bourgeois and reactionary. It was only through dialogue with women at New York's Union Theological Seminary, where she was a visiting professor in the 1970s, that she came to recognize that much of Protestant orthodoxy projects a concept of God that reflected male power over female. She began to question images of God as Lord, Sovereign Power, and patriarchal Father. This God is imaged in terms of power rather than of justice and love. For Dorothee, a "God Almighty" must be rejected in order to discover the "powerless God of Love" that speaks through Jesus Christ. She was fond of saying that "God has no hands but our own."

Today, Dorothee Soelle is recognized as one of twentieth-century Germany's most brilliant theologians. Right before her death, she wrote, "Joy is my most fundamental emotion. It sustains me. The ability to resist, found in a Francis of Assisi or a Martin Luther King, grows with their understanding of beauty. This is the most persistent and the most dangerous form of resistance—that born from being overwhelmed by beauty."

> *As I walk through the valley of this earthly existence,*
> *oh Lord, give me the strength to stand tall. Give me the*
> *courage to question authority when I know in my heart*
> *I am being asked to go against your will. Amen.*

Anne Frank

1929–1945

Indomitable Spirit

I want to go on living even after my death! And therefore I am grateful to God for giving me this gift, this possibility of developing myself and of writing, of expressing all that is in me.

Barely a teen, Anne Frank experienced humanity's worst. For two years, with her family and four others, she survived internal exile in a small warehouse attic. They lived like ghosts, never able to feel the sun on their face or take a deep breath of fresh air. Like so many other Jews in occupied Amsterdam, the captives held on to the hope of escaping death in the concentration camps.

"I can't tell you how oppressive it is never to be able to go outdoors," Anne wrote to "Kitty," her diary. In her isolation, Kitty became her best friend. To her she expressed both fact and feeling: "I'm very afraid that we shall be discovered and be shot. We have to whisper and tread lightly during the day, otherwise the people in the warehouse might hear us."

The quiet magnified the voice of her conscience. Enduring loneliness and the criticism of her companions, she discovered that her faith in God could be a vessel of personal, joyful empowerment:

People who have a religion should be glad. . . . A religion keeps a person on the right path. It isn't the fear of God but the upholding of one's own honor and conscience. . . . You try to improve yourself at the start of each new day. . . . A quiet conscience makes one strong!

From the ages of thirteen to fifteen, when girls awaken to new wonders in life, Anne was closed off from the world. Being cloistered did nothing to interfere with her insatiable curiosity, however. Her spirit began to soar in conditions that would have stifled someone weaker: "I go from one room to the other, breathe through the crack of a closed window. . . . I believe it's spring within me, I feel that spring is awakening, I feel it in my whole body and soul."

However constrained her situation, her deepening relationship with God maintained her faith in the goodness of the universe. She explained to Kitty, "I don't think then of all the misery, but of the beauty that still remains. Look at these things, then you find yourself again, and God."

Although Anne lived long enough to endure terrible suffering and to feel others' pain, she refused to let that dampen her faith in the human spirit. "In spite of everything," she insisted, "I still believe that people are really good at heart. . . . I can feel the suffering of millions and yet, if I look up into the heavens, I think that it will all come out right, that this cruelty too will end, and that peace and tranquility will return again."

Eventually, the inhabitants of "The Secret Annex" were betrayed, arrested, and deported to concentration camps. Anne died of typhus at Bergen-Belsen when she was but fifteen years old. Those who witnessed her living day after day at the camps said that they often saw tears run down her face, washed in compassion at the suffering of others. Her dream to go on "living even after my death" remains true. She is an extraordinary model of the breadth of possibilities inherent in the human spirit.

God, I feel humbled by Anne's courage and compassion. Help me discover strength in my own inner world so that I can embrace my difficulties with faith that You are at work in me transforming the world. Amen.

Maura Clarke

1931–1980

Fidelity

God is very present in His seeming absence.

Maura Clarke loved her work teaching children and training future church leaders. After growing up in Queens, NY, Maura joined the Maryknoll Sisters in 1950 at age nineteen and was assigned to Nicaragua in 1959.

After twenty years of meaningful work in Nicaragua, Maura responded to a call to move to El Salvador, and joined fellow Maryknoll Sister Ita Ford. Consulting local church people about their ministry, Maura and Ita decided to organize relief efforts for rural people suffering human rights abuse in the war-torn province of Chalatenango and to document those abuses. The sisters knew that their advocacy work placed their own lives in danger; they had received death threats, but continued their work with the poor. At that time Maura wrote, "What is happening here is all so impossible, but happening. The endurance of the poor and their faith through this terrible pain is constantly pulling me to a deeper faith response."

The atrocities were horrifying, the terror among the people intense, but Maura stayed. She mused, "My fear of death is being challenged constantly as children, lovely young girls and old people are being shot and some cut up with machetes and bodies thrown by the road and people prohibited from burying them. A loving Father must have a new life of unimaginable joy and peace prepared for these precious unknown, uncelebrated martyrs. One cries out: Lord, how long? And then too what creeps into my mind is the little fear, or big, that when it touches me very personally, will I be faithful?"

Late in November 1980 she and Ita went back to Nicaragua to attend a regional assembly of Maryknoll Sisters in all of Central America. There she affirmed her decision to stay with Ita in El Salvador. She insisted, "God is very present in his seeming absence." Upon her return from the assembly on December 2, she and Ita, along with two other workers, were raped and murdered by members of the El Salvadoran National Guard.

Today, back in her beloved Nicaragua, Maura is known as "the angel of our land." Her name graces schools and homes for battered women and a growing number of girls are being named "Maurita" in her memory.

> *God, when terrible things happen around me or to me,*
> *remind me by the example of Maura's steadfast faith*
> *that You are always with me. Empower me to trust*
> *that You are present even in Your seeming absence.*
> *Amen.*

Beverly W. Harrison

1932–2012

Tender Power

*[T]he power to receive and give love, or to withhold it
. . . is less dramatic, but every bit as awesome, as our
technological power. It is a tender power.*

For scientists, the fundamental element in the universe is the
atom. For ethics scholar Beverly Harrison the fundamental energy
in the universe is relationship. "We are called to a radical activity
of love, to a way of being in the world that deepens relation . . .
Such a perspective enables us to envision our relationship to the
full cosmos."

Beverly Harrison, one of the first prominent women ethicists,
transformed the field. Professor of Ethics at Union Theological
Seminary in New York for thirty-four years, she became the first
woman president of the North American Society of Christian Ethics. Believing that relationships are fundamental to our knowledge
about each other and about God, she developed a "theology of
relation."

Finding and establishing "right relationship" in all areas of our
lives is an intrinsic component of Beverly's theology. The biblical mandate challenges Christians to love without distinction,
as Christ loves, and Beverly Harrison suggested that holding up
the beacon of "right relationship" would illuminate the process

and give us new eyes through which we truly could see. The first step toward building "right-relationship" was to recognize "the aweful, awe-some truth that we have the power through acts of love or lovelessness literally to create one another." Authentic and empathic connection, therefore, was the key to right relationship.

"Because we do not understand love as the power to act-each-other-into-well-being," Beverly cautioned, "we also do not understand the depth of our power to thwart life and to maim each other." Refusing to acknowledge the power we have leads to a terrible desecration of the potential for holiness that relationship holds.

Beverly challenged us to live in ways that allow love to transform us. "Love's work is the deepening and extension of human relations." Jesus is love incarnate. When we open to love, we open to the divine.

> *God of love, may my every interaction with another be burnished by my love for You. Make my relationships a testament to my faith. Amen.*

Genuine Women's Liberation

> *I was led, finally, to say of women's genuine liberation, "This is my struggle. . . ." Once the commitment was clear, my intellectual perspective began to gain a clarity I had never known before.*

As a Christian, Beverly sought to live life as a "joint heir," one who could experience God's love unshackled. She insisted, however, that in order to create the beauty of the kingdom here on earth, we must come face to face with the damage the church has done to women in the name of God. To this end, she dedicated her life to contributing to the work of feminist theology—that is, creating a theology that illuminates biblical texts to empower both women and men to thrive.

Beverly noted, "If women throughout human history have behaved as cautiously and as conventionally as the 'good women' invented by late bourgeois spirituality, if women had acquiesced to 'the cult of true womanhood,' and if the social powerlessness of women, that is the ideal among the European and American 'leisure classes' had prevailed, the gift of human life would long since have faced extinction." Beverly's interest in this subject was, unsurprisingly, personal as well as professional, and born of her own time and place.

Beverly was born in the midst of the Great Depression, a time when, by necessity, women's roles were expanding. As women moved more into territories traditionally held by men, success often meant denying who they were as women. "Because I was acceptable to men and could operate in a 'male' mode, I felt inadequate as a woman. . . . I was simultaneously a professional success and a 'failed' woman."

This gender schism has made women feel less than whole, always at odds in some facet of their lives. "Historically, I believe, women have always exemplified the power of activity over passivity, of experimentation over routinization, of creativity and risk-taking over conventionality. Yet since the nineteenth century we have been taught to believe that women are, by nature, more passive and reactive than men."

Beverly contributed to creating a theological base that allows women their own wholeness—which includes permission to feel their own true feelings. She noted that "Feeling is the basic bodily ingredient that mediates our connectedness to the world. . . . All power, including intellectual power, is rooted in feeling. If we are not perceptive in discerning our feelings, or if we do not know what we feel, we cannot be effective moral agents."

> *God, give me the strength to trust myself and my experience more. Let my God-guided feelings blossom into a full-blown inner voice that acts as my north star, directing me in serving Your plan, doing Your work. Amen.*

Rightly Related to God

> *In biblical terms, the righteous community—the one rightly related to God—is the community that expresses its fidelity to God through concern for the least well-off persons and groups.*

Rugged individualism continues to maintain its iconic hold on our society. Beverly Harrison challenged this paradigm. Her message was simple: To be righteous—that is, "rightly related to God" and in "right relationship" with others—we must measure our lives on how the most marginalized people within our society are or aren't held, supported, and nurtured.

Jesus washed the feet of lepers and broke bread with prostitutes. He exemplified servant leadership, a love so deep it culminated in a willingness to die for his brothers and sisters. In teaching compassion for the broken and outcast, He said, "I tell you the truth, whatever you did not do for one of the least of these, you did not do for me."

According to the Census Bureau in 2002, close to thirty-five million people in the United States were living below the poverty level. That translated to seven million families, or one in every five young children, who did not have enough to eat. Enter the Christian ethic as viewed by theological scholar Beverly Harrison: "A biblical sense of justice focuses on concrete human need. Our sense of justice requires us to make direct address to real, lived-world inequities and to critically scrutinize and protest against institutional arrangements that pervasively perpetuate and deepen social inequities."

According to Beverly, we have three choices: "We can support, and help give birth to, cultural change that is humanly enriching; We can support change that is humanly destructive; or We can, with lack of awareness, seek to prevent change altogether by reinforcing existing convention and practice."

For each of us, the question of how we choose to hearken to this call remains. For Beverly, the first choice was the only option, which meant that all institutions and individuals who aspire to be earthly agents for divine love are morally obligated to act. We are called to build a net of support woven so strategically, that no one in society finds themselves alone on the margins. Beverly offered a powerful summary of her view of the sacred when she insisted, "Passion for justice, shared and embodied, is the form God takes among us in our time."

> *God, I choose to answer the charge! Guide me to*
> *actions I can take that will build on a passion for*
> *justice and make me a vehicle for Your work in our*
> *time. Amen.*

Audre Lorde

1934–1992

Loosening Our Tongues

Your silence will not protect you.

Audre Lorde experienced the triple marginalization of being female, black, and a lesbian. A "sister outsider," she felt the constant
fear of being excluded from her basic civil rights, or, even worse,
suffering physical violence. Deeply acquainted with the temptation
to remain invisible and silent in the face of dread, for "[a]s women
we were raised to fear," Audre exemplifies the courage it takes to
move forward and claim one's voice in the face of intense fear.

Audre Lorde, the third daughter of Caribbean immigrants, was
raised in New York City. Though her severe near-sightedness ren-
dered her legally blind, she learned to read by the age of four, and
soon began writing poetry. Her first published poem appeared in
Seventeen magazine. By the 1960s she was publishing regularly in
Black literary magazines, while also playing an active role in civil
rights and feminist movements. In 1973 she was nominated for the
National Book Award for her book of poems, *From a Land Where
Other People Live*. Still, she struggled to win wider recognition.

Luckily, she had some powerful friends! The wisdom of her ancestors—and divine assistance from God—were on Audre's side. In
her poem "Call," Audre invoked this divine help, praying for the
courage to speak out: "Mother loosen my tongue." Unwilling to be
cowed, Audre made explicit the connection between fear and silence:

In the cause of silence, each one of us draws the face of her own fear—fear of contempt, of censure, or some judgment, or recognition, of challenge, of annihilation. But most of all, I think, we fear the very visibility without which we cannot truly live.

Audre didn't condemn fear, or urge us to rid ourselves of it; instead she encouraged us to speak out despite being afraid. Modeling the courage it takes to speak boldly, Audre used her fear as a propellant. Her willingness to speak out about racial injustice, sexism, and homophobia, inspired a creative relationship between fear and empowerment:

If I cannot banish fear completely, I can learn to count with it less. For then fear becomes not a tyrant against which I waste my energy fighting, but a companion, not particularly desirable, yet one whose knowledge can be useful.

Because she understood how important truth-telling was to spiritual wholeness, Audre invited us "to live beyond fear by living through it" so that we might find our own voice. "When I dare to be powerful, to use my strength in the service of my vision, then it becomes less important whether or not I am unafraid." Audre's poetic call rang out, lighting the darkness. Her courage to voice her pain empowered thousands of others to speak their own truth, even in the face of disapproval or violence.

God of strength, you know that I am human and
afraid. I pray for the courage to speak and act through
my fear and anxiety. Be with me so I can steady my
voice in the struggle for justice. Amen.

Cho Wah Soon

1934–

Fearlessness

Purifying one's inner self through prayer makes one able to see clearly what God's work is.

Some women, like Cho Wah Soon, find that their lives of higher purpose are forged in the fires of early adversity. One of Asia's most powerful social reformers, Cho began her journey of spiritual bravery in the middle of the Korean War.

The civil war between North and South Korea escalated into a multinational conflict when North Korea invaded the South. Tens of thousands of civilians were killed, displaced, and violated in the incursion. Though only sixteen years old, and without formal medical training, Cho was ordered to serve as a field nurse in the army hospital of Pusan. The hospital was filthy, overcrowded, and understaffed. But here, in these horrifying conditions, Cho's spiritual transformation began.

Day by day, Cho became increasingly certain that God was with her, informing her work with divine purpose. She became convinced that as long as she was breathing, her hands could do the work of God. Years later she was able to articulate what this experience gave to her: "I realized God's love through being chosen for this difficult and trying work, and I was born again. No matter how miserable and difficult one's living situation is, if one is awakened to the real meaning of life, it becomes beautiful."

After the war, Cho became a Methodist minister, and to this day she continues working for social justice in South Korea. One story of Cho's life, in particular, demonstrates how she is able to unify her faith and activism.

In 1978, Cho orchestrated a revolt for workers' rights at the Dong-Il Textile Company. When the government leaders learned of her interference, they arrested her. Cho knew from experience that being jailed could lead to torture and even death.

In her memoirs she recalls that in the moment of her greatest fear, she experienced a sudden and complete calm. From within the quiet of that calm, she heard, "When they bring you to be tried . . . do not be worried about how you will defend yourself, or what you will say. For the Holy Spirit will teach you." With these words her fear disappeared. Cho could then joke and raise the spirits of the other workers jailed with her. And when her time finally came, Cho stood with brave resolve to calmly answer her inquisitors:

> Jesus taught that all human beings are created in the image of God. Jesus urged the oppressed to wake up from their oppressed thinking and find their own image. It seems you are calling this rabble-rousing, but if that is so, then Jesus was a rabble-rouser and I—who am trying to resemble him—am also a rabble-rouser. What is wrong with that kind of agitating?

After witnessing her serenity in the face of their insults and threats, the government soldiers released her. Today, it is widely acknowledged that Cho's ministry has changed the course of social history in Asia.

May I keep Cho's story close to me as I face my own fears. Empowered by the same Spirit, may I too ask, "What am I afraid of," when I stand in front of my accusers. Amen.

Mercy Amba Oduyoye

1934–

⌐

Community

*Community is based on the belief that all human
beings are the children of God and are to be honored
and revered.*

"In the religion of the Akans, God is Nana. Some say that Nana
is father, while others say that Nana is mother, but the sentiment
is the same: human beings experience closeness to God which
they describe in terms of motherhood and fatherhood." A member
of the Akan people of Ghana in West Africa and daughter of a
Methodist pastor, Mercy Amba Oduyoye was raised with this very
personal and caring image of God. She brings this experience of
compassion and community to everything she does.

Growing up in Ghana, Mercy's community lived in a quad-
rangle of two big houses, Pramado, and two kitchen houses,
Gyaadze, each with about twelve rooms. The adults were called
elder father, younger father, elder mother, or mother, and the
young ones were all called brother or sister. No one ever went
hungry, everyone shared family concerns, and cooperative econom-
ics helped sustain them. Although many Westerners fear that the
individual does not matter in African communal culture, Mercy
explains, "This is far from the case, as the imperative of mutuality
operates not only between groups but also between individuals.

. . . Mutual caring is central . . . and individuals are encouraged to excel at being caring."

Sharing binds the community together. Families share in ordinary meals, bringing together all ancestors, seen and unseen. Rituals that mark life's passages extend beyond the nuclear family into the whole community. As Mercy writes, "We share our struggles and triumphs, and in doing this we encounter the presence of God among us."

A spokeswoman for the unique contribution of African women to the development of Christian theology, Mercy earned an advanced degree in theology from Cambridge University in England. During the 1990s, she received several honorary doctorates in recognition of her important contributions and accomplishments. She is a founding member of the Circle of Concerned African Women Theologians and is the Director of the Institute of Women in Religion and Culture at Trinity Theological College in Accra, Ghana. She was the first African woman to become a member of the World Council of Church's Commission on Faith and Order.

"African women live by a spirituality of resistance which enables them to transform death into life and to open the way to the reconstruction of a compassionate world. African women live by a resurrection motif." She also notes, "In Africa, spirituality was never lost, so we do not need to organize a search for it."

Loving God, you who have created me as part of a whole, help us to care for the community by caring for its members, and to care for its members by caring for the community, all in your name. Amen.

Rosemary Radford Ruether

1936–

The Full Humanity of Women

Whatever denies, diminishes, or distorts the full humanity of women is . . . to be appraised as not redemptive.

Rosemary Radford Ruether grew up in a devoted and free-thinking Catholic home. In college and graduate school, she studied classics and the social and intellectual history of Christianity. She then became active in the civil rights movement and started teaching in the seminary of a historically black university. From her wide-ranging academic interests and social activism, she has forged a theology based on prophetic visions of justice.

While Rosemary was working against racism and economic injustice in the mid-1960s, she also began raising the issue of sexism, both within the civil rights movement and the church. But as a white woman among an all-male faculty and largely male student body, she was called self-centered and a racist. She was asked by the dean to apologize for her attempt to raise the issue of gender discrimination. She soon began to develop her feminist theology elsewhere.

Rosemary began to catalyze a whole new vision for the church. She was one of the first theologians to start languaging the exclusion and diminishment of women in the history of the church and society at large. She described the church as favoring male privilege, justified in part by long-standing views of women as inferior—or worse—as evil.

Rosemary believes that "the subjugation of women was not God's intent but represent[s] the sinful distortion of human nature by sin." We are all created in the image of God, and we are all equally beloved and essential parts of the sacred creation of life. She insists that "any principle of religion or society that marginalizes one group of persons as less than fully human diminishes us all." Therefore, just as women—and men—come to reject the sexism and misogyny that diminish them, so, too, must they name all related forms of discrimination as unfaithful to the will of God. Rosemary's special attention to prejudice against women is her way of bringing a faithful challenge to the status quo and working toward greater freedom for all of God's creation.

> *God, help me to search my heart, that I may find*
> *imprinted there Your infinite love for all people. And*
> *in so finding, give me a burning desire to seek just and*
> *loving relations with all of your creation. Amen.*

A Prophetic Voice for Justice

> *I don't like injustice and I don't like to see religion used*
> *to justify injustice and oppression.*

A pioneer Christian feminist theologian for over three decades, Rosemary is among the most widely read feminist theologians in North America. Author of over thirty books, including *Sexism and*

God-Talk and hundreds of articles, she served as Georgia Harkness Professor of Applied Theology at the Garrett-Evangelical Theological Seminary in Evanston, Illinois, for twenty-five years, before joining the faculty of Claremont School of Theology in California.

In addition to her work on women and the church, Rosemary has also addressed such topics as the church's anti-Semitism, its participation in ecological destruction, abuses within the Catholic Church, and the Israeli-Palestinian conflict. Rosemary believes that humans and their institutions tend to guard their privilege at the expense of others and even to justify doing so as God's will.

Still deeply committed to the church, Rosemary relies on the prophetic voice of biblical faith, found in the Hebrew prophets and Jesus's life and words, to critique dominant and oppressive structures of power, wherever they are found, while some traditions portray God as putting a divine seal of approval on the status quo of social relations.

> In the prophetic perspective, God speaks through the prophet or prophetess as critic, rather than sanctifier, of the status quo. God's will is revealed as standing in judgment upon the injustices of the way society is being conducted. . . . The spokesperson of God denounces the way in which religion is misused to countenance injustice and to turn away the eyes of the pious from the poor.

If we can acknowledge that the church, like individuals, is subject to both sin and grace, we can begin to recognize our mistakes and set them right. Instead of distracting ourselves from the call to justice by focusing on the sins of others, we are called to live by faith in God who offers forgiveness and redemption for our failings:

God's redeeming presence is at the same time the power to face and shake off the way we cling to privilege and self-deception. We can look steadily and without any denial at the [church's failures], not as the defeat of the gospel, but as the revelation of God's amazing power to deliver us from even our most monumental efforts to defeat God's grace.

In spite of the errors of the institutional church, Rosemary believes that "breakthroughs of authentic love, justice, mutuality, and reconciliation are constantly there also." While some have left the church in dismay at its failings, she has chosen to remain and fight for justice within the Christian community by following the lead of Jesus and the Prophets, and she invites us to join her in this continuing pursuit.

> *Merciful God, help me look beyond my own claims*
> *of righteousness to a higher justice that decries selfish*
> *privilege and power and humbly seeks your grace.*
> *Amen.*

—

Embodied Ecofeminism

Domination of women has provided a key link, both
socially and symbolically, to the domination of earth.

In recent decades, Rosemary Radford Ruether, one of the mothers of contemporary feminist theology, has moved toward ecofeminism. She believes that a healed relation to each other and to the earth calls for a new consciousness. In her book *Gaia & God: An Ecofeminist Theology of Earth Healing*, she has explored the link between the subjugation of women and the rape of the earth.

The central question for Rosemary is "how do we heal the human community from its sexism and its alienation from the rest of nature?" The natural and human community of and on earth is the "sustaining matrix" of all life. Humans are accountable to God for the well-being of all that dwells on earth—other humans, animals, the soil itself. This is not just a nice idea, but rather a covenantal ethic. In order to truly live out this covenant with God, we need a sacramental cosmology—one that truly upholds the sustaining matrix as sacred—which Rosemary finds in both the Jewish wisdom tradition and in a cosmic Christology found in the New Testament.

In these traditions Rosemary discovers a deep respect for the body not simply as a human body, but as the whole body of the cosmos that sustains us. The God in whom we live is not some detached spiritual being in heaven, but rather the one who is in and through and under the whole life process. This voice of God speaks from the intimate heart of matter. It has long been silenced by the masculine voice, but is once again finding her own voice. Her voice does not translate into laws or intellectual knowledge but beckons us into communion.

This more feminine face of God does not rule out the need for a more traditional voice, "one [that] speaks from the mountaintops in the thunderous masculine tones of 'thou shalt' and 'thou shalt not.'" This is the voice of power and law. At its most authentic it speaks out on behalf of the weak, as a mandate to protect the powerless, and to appropriately restrain the power of the mighty. When these two voices of divinity are allowed to complement and balance each other, they contribute to a full experience of all that is sacred within us, our communities, and the world around us.

Rosemary invites us to live within the web of life as sustainers, not as destroyers. "Our kinship with all earth creatures is global.

. . . It also spans the ages, linking our material substance with all the beings that have gone before us on earth and even to the dust of exploding stars."

> *God, font from which all life blossoms forth, give me*
> *the wisdom to live fully within the great web of life.*
> *May I, like Rosemary, recognize my belonging as part*
> *of the whole Earth community. Amen.*

Sister Joan Chittister

1936–

———

The Prophet of Peace

I believe that I'm called by God to keep God a constant question in the human heart.

In every generation, prophets are raised up among us. A prophet of our time, Benedictine Sister Joan Chittister—in her books, speeches, and weekly columns—stands as a torch to light the way for the rest of us. Her message is urgent.

One of her most impassioned warnings focuses on war. We make war differently now, she points out. We don't just kill soldiers, we kill everyone. "War is much more than military conflict now. It is social annihilation. It is the displacement of the innocent, the destruction of the beautiful, the defilement of the holy and the disfigurement of the souls of the young, wounds from which the human spirit never wholly recovers unless and until religion rediscovers spirituality."

Women and children suffer especially. "Women are the booty of war. Their bodies have become the instrument of war. Their children have become the fodder of war." Even as Sister Joan acknowledges women's victimization, however, she empowers them by calling upon their life-giving nature to lead the way to peace. "It's time for women to take as much responsibility for maintaining the life of the world as they do for burying the life of the world."

To make sure we hear what she is saying, Sister Joan uses stories to reach our hearts as well as our minds. Information alone isn't enough to move us. We must connect with our faith, through stories, to gain the courage our challenges require.

"Holy one," the disciples ask, "what's the difference between knowledge and enlightenment?"

The holy one replied, "When you have knowledge, you light a torch to find a way. When you have enlightenment, you become a torch to show the way."

"It's time for women to take their place in bringing spiritual light, to show the world the way the world is adoring the god of death at their expense, at the cost of their children, at the destruction of the globe."

Sister Joan believes that every woman, no matter her circumstances, can become a torch for peace. Every woman can be like the first Jew who stepped into the dry bed of the Red Sea, determined and courageous. "To be holy, we must each take whatever deluge we have in our own lives or together, whatever title wave of distress we are drowning in right now, we must be the first to take that step into the sea." May we heed her words and walk in faith to the Promised Land.

> *Great God of life, let me hear our prophet that I may burn hot with outrage at the violence around us. Let my faith give me courage. Let me be the first to walk into the sea of peace and justice. Amen.*

The Sunflower of Hope

Hope . . . takes life on its own terms, knows that
whatever happens God lives in it, and expects that,
whatever its twists and turns, it will ultimately yield
its good.

A profound thinker who writes with the gripping prose of a novelist, Sister Joan Chittister's writings have influenced millions of people of all faiths. Her own experiences become the springboard for exploring the most important concepts in Christianity, drawing readers into the look, feel, and tension of her human story.

Illuminating how our beliefs shape our outcomes in life, an example of this from Sister Joan's life is her belief in a merciful God, which has allowed her to meet personal loss with the conviction of hidden blessings. In suffering, she sees the invitation to say yes to life, and to choose hope over despair:

The sunflower, that plant which in shadow turns its head relentlessly toward the sun, is the patron saint of those in despair. When darkness descends on the soul, it is time, like the sunflower, to go looking for whatever good thing in life there is that can bring us comfort.

Sister Joan became acquainted with suffering at a very young age when her father died, leaving her and her mother alone. Later, after she found her vocation and her spiritual home with the Benedictine Sisters of Erie, her mother developed Alzheimer's disease. For twenty-eight years, in the face of advancing illness, Sister Joan cared for her.

The death of her father and her mother's illness are mysteries to

Sister Joan, ones she cannot understand in logical terms. In them she finds God's unfathomable grace. "It's not always possible to rejoice in our struggles. But it is always possible to trust them. Then, we may surely give thanks, not for the blessings we have, but for the blessings we cannot see."

Hope conditions us to find the grace that God offers us in every circumstance. We find this hope in our power to believe that God is "lavishing life upon us." It lives in our power to plant more sunflowers in our garden. These patron saints of those in despair will relentlessly remind us to turn toward the sun, no matter the level of darkness we experience.

> *God of hope, be alive in the garden of our hearts. Take root in the soil of our belief. Flourish with beauty, turning my face relentlessly toward the sun. My life demands it. Amen.*

Meinrad Craighead

1936–2019

Art as Ritual

I view my creative work as a continuation of the original gift-giving. I do not know any other definition of "religious art."

When Meinrad Craighead was young, her family moved from town to town and her experience as the "new kid in class" spanned four states. But each summer Meinrad found stability back in Little Rock, where she was born. In her grandparents' small clapboard home on Main Street, she spent every summer reconnecting to her roots and basking in the warm embrace of her beloved "Memaw."

Memaw was a storyteller, and Meinrad spent hours wrapped in her arms on the porch swing listening to the rhythms of her voice. After her family moved from Little Rock to Chicago, Meinrad began drawing. Separated from Memaw, she sent drawings to her and found in art a way to soften her sense of loss. This was her original gift giving, and so began her life as a religious artist (which included fourteen years as a Benedictine nun).

In the years since, Meinrad uncovered many kinds of connections through her drawings and paintings: connections to her biological and spiritual foremothers, to God, to herself, and to the earth and its creatures. Her paintings often include images of sacred women, who may be family members, saints, or even herself.

These women are frequently surrounded by watchful animals, in whom Meinrad found both beauty and spiritual companionship.

For Meinrad, art was both earthly and spiritual. She compared the artistic process to the transformation of a compost heap: "It seethes, makes noises, stinks, bubbles, and emits gasses. All of that is transformation. So, when your imagination gets in there, it's growing in the most incredible, rich earth." It is both death and resurrection. Of her own creative process, she wrote, "Repeatedly I know the times . . . when I go to ground. Let me alone, I cry, I need to rot and rise up and say, 'Look, I have fashioned something which has never existed before.'"

This creativity connected her to God. She believed that "artists live a spirituality of epiphanies. . . . Living at the line between the visible and the invisible, we make our images of the Divine . . . and have ever done so." As visionaries, artists retain their sense of wonder at the world, and art becomes a ritual of worship and thanksgiving. As she explained, "When you wonder, you give thanks, and giving thanks is a ritual. Ritual is the need to do beautiful actions with beautiful things in order to say 'thank you' for this divine beauty we all share."

Yet Meinrad believed that creativity is not an exclusive calling for the select few. Rather, she said, "The work of the spirit is in each of us. All we've got to do is just do it. That is the incarnation, that is making the invisible visible." As for the one who spends her life doing art, she may be "the first to see the treasure which has never existed before. But the treasure is never for yourself. You are just the agent to receive it and bring it back."

> *Gracious God, Source of all things good and beautiful,*
> *connect me to the ground of my being and inspire in*
> *me the desire to give the original gift of my creativity to*
> *the world. Amen.*

Reverend Dr. Suzanne Radley Hiatt

1936–2002

The Bishop of Women

We, who are role models, like it or not, have a responsibility to go in new directions and to help our professions change and grow.

As a young girl, Sue Hiatt knew she wanted to be a priest. "I thought it would be fun to march up and down that aisle, talking to people, being helpful to people." Because it didn't seem possible "I put it out of my head and thought about other things girls could do, none of which sounded like much fun."

As she grew older, Sue's childhood dream of becoming an Episcopal priest faded. Callings don't just disappear, however, and this one resurfaced in a very unusual way. One day as an adult, Sue walked into a church, "frankly, to get warm." Of the church, Sue remembers,

> It was empty. . . . I wandered around, and then sat down on a radiator. I thought, 'What am I going to do with my life?' And a voice said, 'You're going to be a priest. It's what you've always wanted to do.' And I thought, 'No, this is a Presbyterian church.' And the voice said, 'That's true, but you're called to be a priest.' That's what you'd say is a true call to the priesthood.

No matter how impossible it seemed, Sue was unwilling to say "no" to her calling again. She enrolled at the Episcopal Theological Seminary. At that time, women were admitted, but not ordained.

After graduation, the smoldering anger she felt at being given the tools of priesthood without the right to assume the office became a full conflagration. Sue had to do something. On July 29, 1974, eleven women, known forever after as the "Philadelphia Eleven," were "irregularly" ordained as Episcopal priests. Sue was not only a member of this group; she was the driving force behind it. She explained: "In retrospect, to have been ordained 'irregularly' is the only way for women to have done it. Our ordination was on our terms, not the church's terms. It was not accepted as a gift from the church but taken as a right from God." It would be two more years before the governing body of the church granted these women what God already had—the right to serve congregations as priests.

Pioneering the ordination of women was only the beginning of Sue's work. Known as "the Bishop of women," Sue dedicated the remainder of her life to mentoring young women in the divinity school where she taught. Sue borrowed a powerful verse from the book of Amos to express her sense of purpose: "Make justice roll down like waters and righteousness like an everflowing stream." True to these prophetic words, the church experienced a mighty river of change under her visionary leadership.

God, I pray that you will move the waters of transformation through me like a river. I want to be filled with the joy of Your powerful love. Amen.

Delores Williams

1937–

A Way Out of No Way

*Faith has taught me to see the miraculous in everyday
life: the miracle of ordinary black women resisting the
evil forces in society that are working to subvert the
creative power and energy my mother and grandmother
taught me that God gave to black women.*

Growing up in an African American community in Louisville,
Kentucky, in the late forties and fifties, Delores Williams learned
early to recognize black women's strength as well as the forces bent
on undermining that strength. Delores was an activist in the civil
rights movement during the sixties. She married, had four children
and then, later in life, went on to do seminary and doctoral studies
at Union Theological Seminary, where she went on to teach, and
became one of the founding mothers of what has become known
as "womanist theology."

For Delores, womanist theology is rooted in the recovery of
the history of black women in the United States—a history of
survival and resistance in the context of the black family and
community. Womanists fiercely identify with the struggle of the
whole black community against oppression. Womanist theology
helps black women see, affirm, and trust the importance of their
lived experiences of relationships, loss, gain, faith, hope, celebra-
tion, and defiance.

She writes: "Many times, as a little girl, I sat in the church pew with my mother or grandmother, and heard the black believers, mostly women, testify about how far they had come by faith. They expressed their belief that God was involved in their history, that God helped them make a way out of no way." For Delores, the greatest truth of black women's survival is that they have worked to hold themselves and their families together with all the energy of their being. They depended on their strength and upon each other. But in the final analysis, they trusted the end result to God, whom they knew would not fail them.

Delores continued to speak with passion about the unrecognized wisdom of black churchwomen who have always expressed the power of the living Spirit in worship and culture. She reminds us that she was schooled "according to a black folk tradition that taught that trouble doesn't last always, that the weak can gain victory over the strong . . . that God is at the helm of human history and that the best standard of excellence is a spiritual relation to life obtained in one's prayerful relation to God."

> *Dear Jesus, the glory of Your Word is in all that I do and all that I experience. You are my rock as well as my inspiration. May my actions meet the standard of Your love. Amen.*

———

The Survival of Hagar

God's response of survival and quality of life to Hagar is God's response of survival and quality of life to

*African American women and mothers of slave descent
struggling to sustain their families with God's help.*

Womanist theologian Delores Williams has held up the Old
Testament story of Hagar to symbolize the painful history of
African American women—and to empower them. Like many
African American women, she is reinterpreting biblical texts that
offer pathways of liberation to black women.

Hagar's story—one scarred by slavery, poverty, sexual and economic exploitation, surrogacy, rape, domestic violence, and single
parenting—exemplifies the problems that black women have faced
throughout the ages. But Hagar's story also gives black women
an image of survival and defiance, a subversive memory of great
power. In Delores's interpretation, Hagar is the first woman in the
Bible to liberate herself from oppressive power structures.

Reading Hagar's story is to evoke a "dangerous memory." Car-
rying the child of Abraham, dismissed by Sarah, who perceives
her as a threat, Hagar flees into the wilderness, where the angel of
Yahweh finds her and promises that her descendants will be too
numerous to be counted. Hagar and her son Ishmael are forced
from their home and driven into the wilderness, but God is with
them in their plight. Hagar's life is the difficult one of a homeless
single mother. But she also experiences an autonomy with God
as her foundation.

Delores believes that Hagar has spoken to generation after
generation of black women because her story carries their own
suffering. The slave woman Hagar, forced to serve as a surrogate
mother, rejected by Abraham and Sarah and forced to manage on
her own, with her infant son, is a model of many African American
families. A lone mother held a family together in spite of poverty

and marginalization. With only God on her side, Hagar, like many black women, goes into the wilderness to make a living for herself and her child—and survives, despite all odds.

> *God, you walked with Hagar through the wilderness*
> *and promised her a people, give us the courage to*
> *challenge all oppression. Give us the gift of true*
> *freedom that comes from our steadfast faith in you.*
> *Amen.*

Ann Ulanov

1938–

⌒

The Feminine in Jesus

Jesus as human is male, yet he is also bearer of a
large female component, reasonably enough, for Jesus
as Christ presides over all that lives in us, male and
female.

Ann Ulanov invites us into the depths of the human experience, bringing us face-to-face with our inherent paradoxes. This may be uncomfortable at times. But it also enables us to see the contradictions that society as a whole often refuses to make visible. As a Professor of Psychiatry and Religion at Union Theological Seminary in New York, and as a Jungian therapist, Ann invites us to embrace the totality of our being, a totality that includes the dark as well as the light. She has written about Jesus as more than a human man and a divine son. We must be able to experience the feminine in him also.

Few theologians write about Jesus through the lens of his foremothers. However, Ann sees the profound relevance of their inclusion in Christian history. In her book *Female Ancestors of Christ,* Ann asserts, "If we know who our ancestors are, we can live in unbroken continuity with the past. That in turn grounds us in the present." She therefore seeks and finds the women who shaped Jesus's life and the feminine spirit within him.

Ann looks at the five women in Jesus's genealogy—Tamar, Rahab, Ruth, Bathsheba, and Mary—women who are scandalous and yet self-confident, tricky, and also vital and single-minded, and "always in some way related to the joining of sexuality and spirituality." By standing outside the cultural norms of their time, Jesus's female ancestors prefigured his capacity to embrace what had before been outcast, heretical:

> From such intact women comes the Son whose origin and purpose are transcendent, outside manmade customs, fulfilling the spirit of the law by breaking its letter. These women are chaste in the sense of putting first things first and remaining faithful to them.

Ann sees the female ancestry of Jesus as relevant to human needs now because "these women combine what Christian tradition usually separates—the fulfillment of the personal alongside the fulfillment of the holy." Ann seeks to repair a spiritual myopia; she seeks to provide a wide enough lens for the fullness of our human experience to be perceived.

> *Gracious God, you who gave birth to the world, may Your grace give me the courage to embrace the parts of ourselves we have yet to meet. Lift up the feminine in me so that I may recognize myself as reflections of the Eternal Feminine in You. Amen.*

Helen Prejean

1939–

Compassion

*Are we here to persecute our brothers or bring
compassion into the world?*

Jesus never addressed the issue of capital punishment directly.
But he is clear that we shall not kill. His is a hard doctrine. When
the person in question has raped, tortured, and killed innocent
people, perhaps even children, many Christians want to believe
that Jesus would make an exception to his injunction not to kill,
to "love your enemy." Sister Helen Prejean, however, takes Jesus at
his word. "Jesus Christ, whose way of life I try to follow, refused
to meet hate with hate and violence with violence. I pray for the
strength to be like him."

Not only does Sister Helen believe that it is not right to put
convicted murderers to death, but she also believes we must minister to them, as we would any other human being. It makes no
difference how vicious their crimes are, because, she says, "they
are worth more than the worst thing they have ever done in their
lives." Equally important, we must minister to the families of their
victims, enduring their anger that we are caring for the "monsters"
who murdered their loved ones.

Her book *Dead Man Walking*, published in 1993 and later made
into an Oscar-winning movie of the same name, details how her

ministry to death-row inmates emerged. In compelling prose, she describes what it was like to develop relationships with men on death row. She chronicles, in particular, her relationships with convicted killers Patrick Sonnier and Robert Willie and her experience witnessing their executions. She writes, "When you are present for someone like that, about to walk from this room to over there where he is going to be killed, the whole gospel gets distilled. Are you for life or are you for death? . . . Are you for vengeance or are you for compassion?"

She never doubted that these men were guilty, but their guilt didn't keep her from engaging them as she believes Jesus would have done. Before seeing Patrick Sonnier strapped down for execution, she said to him, "Look at me. Look at my face. I will be the face of Christ for you when they do this thing."

Our call, Sister Helen believes, is to follow Jesus in the spirit of compassion, to create a space for healing wherever it has been lost or, perhaps, has never before existed.

> *God of compassion, help me discover and know love in the deepest, most hurtful places. Help me let go of the instinct for revenge and retribution. Cleanse my spirit of the hatred that ruins souls. Teach me forgiveness. Amen.*

Ita Ford

1940–1980

—

Passionate Solidarity with the Poor

*I don't know the answers, but I will walk with you,
search with you, be with you.*

Ita Ford was born in Brooklyn, New York, to a close-knit Irish Catholic family. After college, she decided to become a Maryknoll missionary. In 1973, Ita was assigned to Chile and began working in a shantytown on the outskirts of Santiago. Shortly after she arrived, the democratically elected government of Salvador Allende was overthrown in a bloody military coup. In the ensuing years, Ita witnessed firsthand how friends and neighbors were among those swept up by the military, some to be tortured and imprisoned, and others never to be seen again. In 1977, she wrote in her journal:

> The challenge that we live daily is to enter into the paschal mystery with faith. Am I willing to suffer with the people here, the suffering of the powerless? Can I say to my neighbors—I have no solutions to this situation; I don't know the answers, but I will walk with you, search with you, be with you.

In 1980, Ita responded to a request from El Salvador's Archbishop Oscar Romero for experienced Maryknoll missionaries. While en route to this new assignment she heard the shocking news of Romero's assassination. Sister Maura Clarke joined Ita in their work with refugees. A few months later, both she and Maura attended a Central American regional assembly of Maryknoll Sisters in Nicaragua. On the last day, before returning to El Salvador, Ita read a passage from one of the final homilies of the martyred Archbishop Romero:

> "Christ invites us not to fear persecution because, believe me, brothers and sisters, the one who is committed to the poor must run the same fate as the poor, and in El Salvador we know what the fate of the poor signifies: to disappear, be tortured, to be held captive–and to be found dead."

The next day, December 2, Ita and Maura returned to El Salvador, where they were ambushed and then killed by the Salvadoran military.

Ita left behind a chronicle of her passions and her struggles in her journal and letters. In one letter, written shortly before her death to her niece and godchild for her sixteenth birthday, Ita wrote,

> The odds that this note will arrive for your birthday are poor, but know I'm with you as you celebrate 16 big ones . . . The reasons why so many people are being killed are quite complicated, yet there are some clear simple strands. One is that many people have found a meaning to life, to sacrifice, to struggle and even to death! And whether their life spans 16 years or 60 or 90, for them their life has had a purpose. In many ways they are fortunate people. . . . What I am saying is I hope you come to find that which gives life a deep meaning for you. Something worth living for, maybe even worth dying for, something that energizes you, enthuses

you, enables you to keep moving ahead. I can't tell you what it might be. That's for you to find, to choose, to love. I just encourage you to start looking and support you in the search.

May my life have purpose, dear God, and may I, like Ita, find deep meaning and passion in serving the poor and downtrodden. Amen.

Ivone Gebara

1944–

~

Ecofeminism Born
of a Commitment to the Poor

My ecofeminism is pregnant with health: not health as
we understood it in the past, but the health of a future
that promises deeper communion between human
beings and all other living things.

Poor women in Latin America, called to act against their own
oppression and the destruction of the earth, have found a cham-
pion in Ivone Gebara, the region's foremost ecofeminist theologian.

Ivone's ecofeminism is born from the daily injustice she experiences:

> With ecofeminism I have begun to see more clearly how
> much our body—my body and the bodies of my neigh-
> bors—are affected not just by unemployment and economic
> hardship, but also by the harmful effects the system of indus-
> trial exploitation imposes on them. I sense that ecofeminism
> is born of daily life, of day-to-day sharing among people,
> in the streets; bad smells, the absence of sewers and safe
> drinking water, poor nutrition, and inadequate health care.
> This is no new ideology. Rather, it is a different perception
> of reality that starts right from the unjust system in which

we find ourselves, and seeks to overcome it in order to bring happiness to everyone and everything.

A religious sister, Ivone holds doctorates in both philosophy and religious sciences, and she is the author of many books, including her opus on ecofeminism: *Longing for Running Water: Ecofeminism and Liberation* (1999). She also taught epistemology and philosophy in the Catholic Theological Institute in Olindo/Recife for fourteen years.

Though she could be living in a comfortable convent provided by her order, Ivone chose to live in a slum outside Recife in Northeastern Brazil. The daily life of her neighbors, most of whom are poor women, is the locus from which she constructs her theology. Those who attend her courses, or read her books and articles, feel they know her well. This is because Ivone speaks from her own experience, sharing her life and feelings with her audiences so completely that many of her readers consider her a personal friend.

Deeply concerned for the plight of underprivileged women in her community, Ivone's message is clear: do what you must to rise up out of poverty, even if it means ignoring the human dictates of the church. In 1994, Ivone was "silenced" by the Vatican for her unorthodox opinions. Ordered "back to school" for doctoral studies in theology at a Pontifical Catholic University in Europe, she used the time to write another book!

Fiercely compassionate, Ivone insists that ecofeminism's invitation to love and mercy does not come from a reality that is external to us. Rather, it is an urge present in our very humanness. "My ecofeminism is shot through with the staunch conviction that beauty is important in healing people." Ivone invites us to imagine a postpatriarchal world where salvation does indeed come through beauty.

*God of all creation, help me to become ever more
aware of the deep communion between human beings
and all other living things. As I work for justice, may
I not forget that salvation and healing come about
through beauty. Amen.*

Bernice Johnson Reagon

1942–

Wrapping Your Feet around Justice

i say, come wrap your feet around justice
i say, come wrap your tongues around truth
i say, come wrap your hands with deeds and prayer

Bernice Johnson Reagon was birthed into and nurtured by the deep spiritual embrace of the black church. But it wasn't until she began marching for freedom during the civil rights movement that the power of the church ignited within her. "The movement changed my understanding of the church. There were songs that I heard for the first time . . . church songs. The old people who were singing them were singing them out of their lives and their belief. But until I used my life to stand for right, I didn't understand the songs."

Taking action gave Bernice's voice strength for the fight, and she channeled this strength into the world-renowned a cappella group she founded. "Sweet Honey in the Rock" reaches across boundaries of race and class to celebrate the joy and sorrow of the human condition. It rouses the spirit and galvanizes the soul:

> I sing in Sweet Honey
> Because it is a way to be in the world
> Holding ground slipping
> Under my feet

Walking the line of history
Standing at the foundation
And center of the world
Human family

Shouting in joy
When our living lights the heavens
With our love—
And weeping tears
That we still eat our young

Through song, Bernice connects with the challenging darkness and spirited light of her ancestral heritage in a visceral way. There is no single definitive record of how many blacks were lynched during the dark time in our history that has been referred to as the Black Holocaust. The outrage Bernice felt as she opened to this generations-old pain brought home the story of Jesus and his crucifixion in a new way. Some accounts say close to 2,400 blacks were killed. Others estimate that, between 1880 and 1920, an average of two African Americans were brutally murdered each week. Bernice wrote, "I actually understood the crucifixion in a different way. I was able, because of the movement, to really understand lynching as a kind of crucifixion."

Wrapping her feet, voice, heart, and soul around justice, Bernice feels herself called both into the pages of history and the experience of the eternal:

Feels like a slice of
Unending
Foreverness
Don't it?

I want to raise my voice in song, as Bernice does. I
want to feel the rhythms of justice and praise, O God,
as I stand with others singing your song. Amen.

—

Singing God

As I gave power to the sound of my own voice
A way broke before me, I followed my choice . . .

The way before me was mine to make
There was no road, no path to take

Stepping outside of her comfort zone, Bernice Johnson Reagon found the power of her own voice. This power enabled her to sing out against the oppression of her people.

In 1961, a group of black students was arrested for trying to purchase tickets from the "white" window at a Trailways Bus station. Though filled with trepidation, Bernice felt compelled to march in their support. "We left the campus and headed out. Maybe there were ten people, so I just kept my face ahead. I knew if I turned around, I would just run back to campus."

Unable to resist, Bernice did turn around, and "as far as I could see, all the way back to campus, there were people. I tell you I never knew where they came from. I never heard them coming." It was a startling realization. At a glance she learned "the power of finding that you can step out and sometimes you'll have company before you get there!"

After circling the jail twice, someone shouted out for Bernice to sing. In this moment Bernice surrendered to God and felt the beginning of her own inner power. Opening her mouth wide, she let her voice soar with the pathos and majesty of the Heavens:

I started "Over My Head" and the spiritual goes, "Over my head / I see trouble in the air." So I flipped trouble into freedom. It was the first time I had ever done that, especially with a sacred song, a spiritual that came from slavery. I realized that there was something about the march that had moved me to a position where I could use the songs I had been taught.

Many of the protestors were arrested, but "the singing in jail went on endlessly," Bernice remembered. After she got out of jail, Bernice found that her voice had changed. "In the first mass meeting, they asked me to sing. I sang the same song, 'Over My Head / I hear Freedom in the Air,' but my voice was totally different. It was bigger than I'd ever heard it before. It had this ringing to it. It filled all the space of the church. I thought that was because I had been to jail; it was because I had stepped outside of my comfort zone."

Since that day, Bernice Johnson Reagon has changed the words to many more spirituals while singing about slavery and freedom to hundreds of thousands of people. Singing to God is her way of unleashing the spirit within her and bringing others to stand and shout for justice:

Wanna rise standing
Wanna rise shouting
Wanna rise singing
Wanna rise fighting
Wanna rise sanctified!

God, You are the music of my soul. Let my voice ring out my protest against tyranny. And the harmonious notes of my song express my job for the justice You demand. Amen.

Elaine Pagels

1943–

———

Facing Death with Faith

*I happened to stop in this church because it was cold,
and I was startled at how moved I was by the worship
in progress. And the thought that came to me was,
"Here's a family that can speak about death."*

When Elaine Pagels heard the diagnosis that her two-year-old
son's illness would ultimately be fatal, she had been away from the
church for many years. Church was not on her mind the next day
either, as she ran her regular route in Central Park in New York
City. It was a cold February morning, and when she stopped at a
cathedral on the edge of the park, it was simply to warm up a little
before she headed home.

As she walked in, she was surprised by her reaction to the
beauty of the architecture and the service. She felt surrounded by
positive energy: "Standing in the back of that church, I recognized
uncomfortably that I needed to be here. Here was a place to weep
without imposing tears on a child." As she watched the liturgy
unfold, she began to feel a sense of ultimate accord: "Perhaps that
is what made the presence of death bearable. Before that time, I
could only ward off what I had heard and felt the day before."

While her body thawed, her soul warmed in the presence of
God. Elaine had found a community that faced death with com-

passion rather than with dogma. She had found a place that "could deal with the terrible needs that we have when we face that kind of vulnerability." Years later, when her son died at the age of six and a half, she returned to the church. "It was there that we went to gather with our friends for a service that could bridge what had seemed to be an absolutely impassable abyss," the loss of an only child.

A year later, Elaine's husband died in a climbing accident in the Rockies. While shaken to the core, she continued to seek the deeper sense of hope and purpose to be found within Christianity. Mindful of the critics who dismiss religious hope as delusion, she believes that "hope actually invents itself, . . . in our lives. And it isn't just a fantasy and a fallacy. . . . one has to go on living."

Elaine is known for being a lightning rod among contemporary biblical scholars. But when her personal foundation was shaken, she found an anchor within the Christian faith. She had discovered an "enormous reservoir of ways to deal with reality. Not just . . . to avoid it, or hide from it. Or fool ourselves. But actually ways to cope with the painful realities of our lives. And actually transform them." She was brought back to her faith in despair and has stayed to offer others the hope and comfort she received when she needed it most.

> *God of life and death, in my darkest hour, you call me*
> *by name. Help me understand the mystery of death*
> *and the promise of life that seems so far away. I am*
> *not alone. You are with me always, especially when my*
> *heart is broken. Amen.*

Ada María Isasi-Díaz

1943–2012

En La Lucha (In the Struggle)

Liberation is a possibility for all if we are willing to struggle.

The raw violence of the Cuban revolution shaped the course of Ada María Isasi-Díaz's life. A teenager when Castro's regime seized political power in her homeland, she fled with her family to the United States in 1960 for asylum. The despair and divisiveness resulting from the oppression of her people catalyzed Ada María's purpose. Early in life she was drawn toward people surviving the darkness of unjust political regimes and policies. As an activist, a professor of ethics at Drew University in New Jersey, and author of books and articles on liberation theology, she has stayed true to her life's purpose. She coined a new term, *mujerista* theology, to express the distinctive experience and perspective of Latina women, whose faith is forged in the struggle against sexism, ethnic prejudice, and economic oppression.

Ada María recognized early on that the multiple injustices Latinas face every day can make them feel powerless. So, Ada María invited them deeper into a living, breathing relationship with their Creator. Knowing God's presence with them as teacher, friend, and comforter "en la lucha," she taught:

Biblical stories help us hold on to the belief that within the limited possibilities we have as marginalized people, one does what is possible. . . . Partial solutions are transformative elements because the struggle to bring them about provides inspiration.

A true feminist liberation theologian, Ada María proclaimed that God will not come alive in theology unless it emerges from real relationships. "I cannot do theology and will not do theology apart from a community of support and accountability." She saw that women will do whatever it takes to stay in the struggle, to be responsible *to* others—not *for* others—allowing them "to hold us accountable for who we are and what we do."

In Ada María's sense of purpose, the struggle itself transforms us. It puts us in touch with God. It builds community. It strengthens us so we are able to bear greater burdens for one another, so we can take on the greater injustice.

The power of her words derives from her determination to include herself in this great dance, moving forward, stumbling, rising up, taking a few more steps:

The struggle is not to go through life bent on not falling. No, the struggle, *la lucha,* is to learn to stand up again. So I preach today not because I have not fallen but because I am willing to do all in my power to stand up again.

God of all things, I want to embrace my difficulties
and not resist them. I want to find you "en la lucha."
I want to dance always toward the promised liberation.
Amen.

China Galland

1944–

―――

Redeeming Darkness

To say that one is "longing for darkness" is to say that one longs for transformation, for a darkness that brings balance, wholeness, integration.

"Addiction steals souls" author China Galland has said of her alcoholism. "Mine had almost been lost." To heal, China turned "psyche inside out, shaking loose all the broken parts." China calls it "claiming our shadow," those parts of ourselves hard for us to see, but very visible to others. China's journey reminds us that working with the shadow requires great depth of courage.

The Black Madonna was touchstone, confidant, and mother to China as she began to journey into the unknown parts of herself. Shrines of these dark images of the Virgin Mary can be found throughout the world. China's articles and book on the meaning of the Black Madonna are a gift to all who seek "a redeeming darkness."

"The association of the word 'darkness' with evil," China insists, must be changed. "The Black Madonnas are very powerful. They carry the wisdom of healing and wholeness." Understanding this "gives us a way to begin to speak to one another about the positive image of darkness."

China shares that she desperately needed the power and healing offered by the Black Madonna. "Being able to stay sober depended upon making a radical change." This included having to "replace my dependence on a substance, something material, with something insubstantial, immaterial. I would have to give up control." The only way China could do this was to "find a way of conceiving of a power greater than myself and a way to improve whatever contact I might have with it."

What China didn't realize at the time was that her greatest weakness would lead to an inexhaustible source of strength: "The disease draws one into an increasing loss of self-respect, to the point where, at the bottom, it is felt that hardly anyone could be more 'contemptible' than oneself. Yet in recovery, the very wound that drains one's life is the greatest source of healing and transformation."

Once China allowed herself to move into her darkness, she was able to claim an inner source of power. By "shaking loose the broken parts" of herself and drawing on the strength of "a fierce Mary, a terrific Mary, a fearsome Mary," China was able "to give up any version of my story in which I depict myself as a victim. . . . and take full responsibility for my life."

> *I pray that you intercede for me as I seek greater*
> *courage to live fully. Looking at the brokenness of my*
> *life, may I learn to embrace all of myself, even areas*
> *where I feel shame and contempt. Amen.*

Carter Heyward

1945–

~

Redemption

To make love is to make justice.

"To what extent," posits Carter Heyward, "are we responsible for our own redemption in history?" Carter was one of feminist theology's foundational scholars. After receiving her Masters of Divinity and PhD in Systematic Theology from Union Theological Seminary in New York, she served for many years as a professor at Episcopal Divinity School in Cambridge, Massachusetts. Grappling with redemption has been a personal, as well as professional, journey; one that has greatly influenced her experience and understanding of theology. She does not believe in the traditional notions that " 'redemption' is God's act of lifting us above ourselves, a process of divine deliverance from the human condition."

In Jesus, she asks us not to see one who "sits high above humanity," but rather a Jesus "who despised the notion of a deity who likes sacrifice, especially human sacrifice." She asks us "to re-imagine a Jesus whose love for God was entwined with his love for humanity; a Jesus whose ethical norm was that to love God is to love our neighbors as ourselves. To love God is to effect right relation, justice, among human beings. To act with God by God and for God must include the commitment to act with humanity, for humanity, by human choice. To love God is to love humanity so intimately that the realm of God is known to be here and now among lovers of humanity."

And if we imagine ourselves participating with Christ in the world, it may sometimes mean to suffer with one another, "I am learning that, as a process of liberation from either injustice or despair, healing is a process of finding—if need be creating—redemption in suffering." Yet she does not believe in "'redemptive suffering' as a means of justifying either pain or God," but rather "in the midst of suffering, we weave our redemption out of solidarity and compassion, struggle and hope. In this way, we participate in the redemption of God." For Carter sees that "if there is to be any redemption of humanity from evil in the world, it is up to us. We can never again abdicate our responsibility to an omnipotent deity. If only we take humanity seriously on humanity's terms may God be delivered, with us, from evil."

All-knowing God, may I find in love the power and
the courage to re-create the world. Amen.

―

Theology of Mutuality

God is . . . the eternally creative source
of our relational power . . .
a god whose name in history is love.

There is a kind of theology that emphasizes the ways in which God is distant from humanity. In this view, God is magnificent and awesome and we are lowly and powerless. Carter Heyward has a different view. She asserts that in experiencing God, the Spirit lives within us and our everyday actions. That God's love wants to become manifest in our very lives: "If we fall into the likeness of God . . . then we are co-creators . . . in the world."

As an early pioneer in feminist theology, Carter insists that much of the Spirit of God "is our power in relation to each other, all humanity and creation itself." She says,

> There is something basic among us, something evolutionary—and revolutionary; something more basic than femaleness or maleness, whiteness or blackness, gayness or straightness: something more basic than Christianity or any religion. I am speaking of the human experience, and perhaps also the experience of other creatures, of love—or, of our human experience of God in the world.

In the mid-1980s, Carter traveled with a group of seminary-based educators and students to Nicaragua. She witnessed community-based relationships in which "No one is left out of either the benefits or the responsibilities of living in a relation of love toward the neighbor." She realized the power of creating strong relationships and bonds with others: "We are never called forth alone but always to answer the Spirit's call with one another . . . at the core of our faith, we know that in the beginning and in the end, we are not alone. In our living and in our dying, we are not separate from one another."

And it is through this very present and real connection with others that she encounters the divine. For Carter "when we are most fully in touch with one another . . . we are participants in ongoing incarnation, bringing God to life in the world." For she sees that a God who is in relation is one "who reaches and is reached, touches and is touched, empowers and is empowered."

> *Loving Creator, help me remember that to reach out*
> *and care for others is to reach out and touch the*
> *Divine. Amen.*

Diana Eck

1946–

Religious Pluralism

*The ways of seeing the divine are limited not by God's
capacity to be present, but by our human capacity
to see.*

Diana Eck's Christian faith is enhanced by its encounter with
religious diversity. As Professor of Comparative Religion at Harvard and the director of the Pluralism Project, Diana has committed her life to conveying the message that, "not only must we learn
to live with other worldviews, but we are enriched when we do."

Diana traveled far from her roots in Bozeman, Montana. The
world of religious diversity opened up for Diana in 1965 during an
undergraduate trip to Banares to study India's many faces of God.
She was well steeped in the core of her own Christian faith: "love,
justice, human dignity, and the steady sense of being linked in kinship to Christ and the Christian community." But she knew little
of other faiths. Confronted by the teeming mass of humanity, the
musky and sharp smells of curry and cumin, the overwhelming poverty and the eclectic mix of sacred and profane in India, Diana had
an *aha moment*. "I realized that to speak of Christ and the meaning
of incarnation might mean being radically open to the possibility
that God encounters us in the lives of people of other faiths."

The variety of religious and cultural differences is staggering.
In her book *A New Religious America,* Diana notes that there

are currently more than three hundred Buddhist temples in Los Angeles, home to the greatest variety of Buddhists in the world. And there are more American Muslims than there are American Episcopalians, Jews, or Presbyterians. Peace in the world depends greatly on our capacity for religious tolerance and understanding.

Through her own faith as a Methodist Christian and her scholarship of world religions, Diana demonstrates that diversity can strengthen rather than spark controversy and violence. Her encounter with other religions has made the mystery of God real for her. Only by embodying a profound humility can we reach the steadfast core of our own faith. "Being a Christian pluralist means daring to encounter people of different faith traditions and defining my faith not by its borders, but by its roots."

In this way, different faiths become a God-given opportunity to grow in our relationships with one another. There is an ancient Hindu belief that God appears to people in the way that will enlighten and serve them most. Perhaps then, as Diana's work suggests, the many faces of God in our world can be seen as our greatest gift as well as our greatest challenge. Religious diversity asks that we might extend beyond our individual understanding of God and seek to understand others as well—all for the sake of allowing our faith to bring us closer, rather than tearing us apart. This is the hard-won treasure Diana offers to us in her work with Pluralism, the chance to see the wisdom in the Muslim belief that "God has made us into many races and families and tribes so that we may know each other. But that difference is not a threat to us. Difference is an opportunity for understanding."

Great and mysterious God, I pray to you using Diana's words: "Open my eyes. Let me try to understand what it means to speak of the many-ness of God." Amen.

Hanan Ashrawi

1946–

⁓

Bearing Witness and Speaking Out

*A genuine leadership does not disempower half its
people, and real women do not accept exclusion and
internal alienation.*

That rare combination of politician and poet, Hanan Ashrawi
broke on to the global scene in 1988 during an interview between
Israelis and Palestinians on ABC's *Nightline*. To a world that too
easily identified Palestinians as backwards rock throwers, this brilliant, articulate, pragmatic—and Anglican Christian—woman
surprised the world.

Hanan was born in the city of Nablus in the region of Tiberias
in 1946, two years before the formation of the state of Israel. Her
family was forced to relocate to Ramallah during the subsequent
reconfiguring of Palestine. Hanan's father, a fearless advocate for
human rights, spent four years in an Israeli jail. But he always
told Hanan, "We raised you not to feel in any way that you are
handicapped by your gender or your upbringing, so . . . do things
on issues of justice and what you believe in."

Hanan responded by completing a doctorate in medieval literature at the University of Virginia. She was teaching at Bir Zeit University in Palestine, when Yasser Arafat, chairman of the Palestinian
Liberation Organization, appointed her as the official spokesperson

of the Palestinian delegation to the Middle East Peace Process. And political pundits took notice when she trounced her debate partner Benjamin Netanyahu, who would later become Israel's prime minister, on the issue of Palestinian independence.

In 1990, Hanan founded an independent human rights organization called the Palestinian Initiative for the Promotion of Global Dialogue and Democracy. From this base she traveled the world, educating people on the realities of Palestinians, the politics of the Middle East, and how a values-based peace might be achieved in the region. "Peace cannot be an artificially imposed quiet held in place by subjugation and suffering," she said. "There is no peace based on the weakness of the victim."

Hanan's faith and compassion have not withered in the harsh cauldron of politics and suffering. While she has the wisdom of the serpent in the political sphere, she has the gentleness of the dove in her poetry, which reflects her people's agony and joy. "Areej," she writes in the poem "Areej the Scent of Youth and Death," "the fragrance of wild flowers / Wafting through the hills of Hebron, yours / Is no abstract death / And mine is no impersonal sorrow." When asked how people of faith could help her work, the answer was simple. "Caritas. Charity. Show us basic human compassion in our suffering," she said. "Bear witness and speak out."

> *Sharpen my mind, Lord, that I may use it as the sword of your truth. Like Hanan, let my heart be soft for those who suffer and my strength be fierce is pursuit of justice.*

Jane Kenyon

1947–1995

—

Hope in the Face of Suffering

The poet's job is to tell the whole truth and nothing but the truth, in such a beautiful way that people cannot live without it.

When poet Jane Kenyon was diagnosed with leukemia, she felt her world shattering. In her early forties, she was deeply in love and beginning to receive recognition as one of the nation's finest poets. The sudden diagnosis plunged her into the depths of depression, extinguishing her poetic fire. Eventually, the poet in her was too strong to be silenced. Jane was able to go within and forge a deeper path, one that ultimately brought more light into the world. Her own suffering made her exquisitely aware of the intricacies of life. She learned how wonder can be experienced in the midst of fear.

In her poem "Notes from the Other Side," you can hear her acceptance of death and her faith that what we are left with at the end, after everything else has gone, is God's love. As her own death drew nearer, and as she "divested" herself of fear, she wrote, "Our calm hearts strike only the hour, / and God, as promised, proves / to be mercy clothed in light."

In another poem, Jane asserts that happiness is like the prodigal son, who seems to abandon us and then turns up, unexpectedly.

When it seems most unlikely, Joy comes in a more deeply felt form than ever before:

> You make a feast in honor of what was lost, and
> take from its place the finest garment, which you
> saved for an occasion you could not imagine, and
> you weep night and day to know that you were not
> abandoned, that happiness saved its most extreme
> form for you alone.

Jane used words to transform her pain into truths that were larger than her individual suffering. When she realized she was going to die, she collected certain poems for an anthology to be titled *Otherwise*. Published posthumously, this was her final, intensely personal gift to those of us who are trying to reconcile the love and dying that are present in our own lives.

As Jane saw it, no matter what happens to any of us, "we have the consolation of beauty, of one soul extending to another soul and saying, 'I've been there too.'"

> *Oh God, I am only human. If I fall ill like Jane, and*
> *grieve, and wish life were otherwise, open my heart to*
> *the truth, that I am never alone and without hope.*
> *Amen.*

Julia Cameron

1948–

⌒

Creativity

Art is a spiritual transaction.

"Humbled by the power of God, the Great Creator, to restore strength, vitality, and inspiration to individual creative paths," Julia Cameron has been a prolific writer for over thirty years. Her willingness to bare her soul so that others could connect with their own creativity transformed her into a spiritual mentor to creative people the world over.

Though Julia had enjoyed success as a writer in her twenties, a drinking problem caused her writing to come in bursts. Of this unreliable writing, Julia recalled, "If creativity was spiritual in any sense, it was only in its resemblance to a crucifixion." But what was the alternative? She knew continued drinking would kill her. But what if stopping caused her creative well to dry up completely? She made the only decision she could: to stop—not knowing that such a decision would be the necessary beginning to a new and enduring creative journey.

With her sudden sobriety, Julia surrendered herself—mind, body, psyche, muse, et al.—over "to the only god I could believe in, the god of creativity." Getting out of her own way, she opened herself up to the creative forces at work within her, and—to her immense relief—began writing freely. Her writing focus was deceptively simple: show up for the process, but let go of the result. In doing so, Julia learned that it was her job to write and God's job to worry about the outcome. The more she let go, the easier—and more joyfully—her writing came. It wasn't long before one of her artist friends asked for help. And then another.

On one of her afternoon walks along the Hudson River, Julia heard the explicit call to formalize what she was already doing informally: to share her gifts and experience through teaching. One week later she had a teaching job, and was helping artists she'd never met before get out of their own way and trust in a Creator God. Her classes and workshops culminated in her book *The Artist's Way*. Ideas from this groundbreaking book on opening up the creative process are being used in hospitals, schools, prisons, battered women's shelters—anyplace where people seek healing and wholeness. By offering her process out into the world, Julia felt herself becoming "a spiritual conduit for the central spiritual fact that the Great Creator loved other artists and actively helped those who opened themselves to their creativity."

Julia generously encourages others to make use of her ideas, for she believes that "creativity is an act of faith, and we must be faithful to that faith, willing to share it to help others, and to be helped in return." She has come to understand and teach that creativity is a natural part of who we are as God's creatures, that by "opening our souls to what must be made, we meet our Maker."

> *Creator God, help me get out of my own way and embrace my creativity as a spiritual gift, one to be shared abundantly with others. Let me feel Your presence in every creative act. Amen.*

Art as Faith

Leap, and the net will appear.

The words that open this entry are taped to Julia's writing desk, encouraging her to continuously take the plunge into the world of creative expression. Experience has taught her that this gesture of faith will be met with divine support. True art, Julie has discovered, is fundamentally an act of faith and courage.

Creative people are plagued by "blocks": worry that they lack vision, doubt that they can manifest their vision on canvas or page, worries about income, feelings of selfishness, fear of failure and/or fear of success (sometimes on the same day!). Some of these blocks come from wrong-headed cultural ideas about the practice of art, others from childhood experiences of shame. They can grow into powerful obstacles to creativity. Overcoming these demons requires both the willingness to face old fears and trust in our Creator to embrace and sustain us in the struggle. In healing the wounds that have alienated us from our true selves, we become, as if for the first time, whole spiritual and psychological beings.

Leaping is the first step in this process. We have to write, paint, dance, sing, and commit to our creative work before we actually see any positive results of our engagement. In faith we must begin to pursue our dreams before we know where the pursuit will take us. "Our creative dreams and yearnings come from a divine source. As we move toward our dreams, we move toward our divinity." Julia reminds us that just as God is the source of our dreams, so too, "God has the power to accomplish them."

When we start to nurture our creativity, we begin "to forge a creative alliance, artist-to-artist, with the Great Creator," to let God's creativity flow through us. Our initial act of trust develops into an attitude of trust, making more and more achievements possible. We gain faith in the Great Creator and the creator within, and soon we find it easier to exercise our creativity than to withhold it. "You will learn to enjoy the process of being a creative channel and to surrender your need to control the result." Blocks of fear, uncertainty, and shame give way to delight, ease, and playfulness.

In a strong antidote to the negative beliefs that thwart human creativity, Julia insists that refusing to be creative is "counter to our true nature." She urges us to cling instead to divine reciprocity: "Creativity is God's gift to us. Using our creativity is our gift back to God." Then, as we heal ourselves, we offer hope to others and a treasure to the world.

> *God of all creativity, you celebrate me as a fellow artist!*
> *Grant me the courage to follow Julia and take the leap*
> *that brings my gift to life in the world. Amen.*

Adele Ahlberg Calhoun

1949–

Holding Paradoxes

We keep company with Jesus by making space for him through a spiritual discipline. Our part is to offer ourselves lovingly and obediently to God.

Adele Ahlberg Calhoun's desire to hold the paradoxes that lead to spiritual integration began with seismic shifts in the church. As a young adult, she began to notice different ways people expressed their faith: different denominations, different movements—neo-evangelicals, charismatics, megachurches, televangelists, as well as those engaged in movements for social change and reform. She raised the question, "What does it look like to follow Jesus? How do I actually LOVE God, neighbor, and self with all my head intelligence (IQ), my heart intelligence (EQ) and my gut/body strength intelligence (GQ)?"

Curiosity and the desire to love God, and a passion to see others live the glory of their divine image, fueled Adele's calling to become a pastor, professor, spiritual director, author, pilgrimage leader, icon writer, and retreat speaker. Her roles have created space for others to explore who God is and how the Spirit of God moves in thoughts, emotions, instincts, and our moment in history.

Adele has worked in Christian ministry for over forty years. She is currently co-pastor, with her husband, Doug, of Redeemer Community Church in Needham, Massachusetts. She is the author of *Spiritual Disciplines Handbook, Invitations from God*, and coauthor of *True You: Overcoming Self-Doubt and Using Your Voice.* A trained spiritual director, she has taught courses at Wheaton College and Northern Baptist Theological Seminary.

Her book *The Spiritual Disciplines Handbook* invites people to notice God-given desires and how they point to practices that can transform them. In leading workshops on the enneagram, a model for understanding personality types, she invites people to explore transformative work in personal, relational, institutional, and systemic contexts. She has elaborated on these life-giving principles in *Spiritual Rhythms for the Enneagram: A Handbook for Harmony and Transformation.*

Adele wanted eyes to see the glory in all human beings, and how "everything belonged." In her work she shows us the way to explore multifaceted ideas, while holding God in our hearts. Jesus, she believes, embodied paradox. He was divine and human! He was powerful and vulnerable! He was full of grace and truth.

Adele teaches us to use all our inherent tools even while we may experience discomfort on holding two opposing views at once. For her, a life of faith includes doubt. It includes inner and outer spirituality, being and doing, contemplation and action, practice and belief, beauty and truth, and objectivity and subjectivity. It includes a way of knowing that draws on the head, the heart, and the gut.

> *Heavenly Father, I am before You. I delight in the paradoxes you provide so that we may know you in profound ways. Enlighten the eyes of our heart that we might see you and notice how you're at work through our lives. Amen.*

Bernadette Cozart

1949–2009

—

A Green Revolution

*If you can take a garbage-strewn lot . . . and turn it
into a thing of beauty that benefits the community—a
thing of usefulness—then you know you can transform
other things. You can transform things you don't like in
your own life and in yourself—and that's power.*

When Bernadette Cozart looked at the streets of Harlem, she
didn't see the trash littering the curbs. A gardener for the Parks
and Recreation Department of New York City, and founder of the
Greening Harlem Coalition, Bernadette could see

> vacant lots as sources of jobs. I can see growing vegetables
> and herbs . . . going all the way from seed to shelf. I envision
> watermelon rind jelly, tomato preserves, and "cha cha" with
> labels that say "grown and made in Harlem."

One day she was working on a garden in New York, and a group
of teens began following her around. Inspired, she handed each
of them a shovel, showed them an area with bare dirt, pointed to
flats of flowers, and told them to create a flower garden. "They did
a great job. I thought it would be a grand idea if they could do
parks in their own neighborhood." And the idea for the Greening
of Harlem Coalition was born.

The garden, for Bernadette, was metaphor and manifestation, representing the myriad possibilities when people joined together, investing sweat equity in a common goal. One could say that she saw God in gardens, because divinity often emerges wherever people are connected in a common creation.

Churches call people into being of service to their community. And planting a garden can, too. Prisoners, battered women, the deaf, Vietnam veterans, children, ministers, teachers, and people who are HIV positive work alongside one another, pitching in to create an urban oasis. "They are learning to nourish the garden," Bernadette reflected, "and nourish each other. "

Because of Bernadette, over thirty neighborhood gardens arose in Harlem, built and maintained by local residents. Each new garden nurtures the soul and instills pride and self-respect in the people who live there. Bernadette called this "the power of transformation through gardening. It gives people a hope that is desperately missing." It's a source of pride in Harlem—that among the beauty of marigolds and green beans, hope is also flowering.

> *God, help me to cultivate the seeds of beauty and hope*
> *in my own heart so that I may grow into one who*
> *nurtures the spirits of all who live in my community.*
> *Amen.*

Deborah Lindholm

1949–

~

Miracles Happen

If you empower a man, you empower one person. If you empower a woman, you empower her entire family. When women get together, miracles happen.

Deborah Lindholm has wanted to transform the way women around the world provide for their families. Her faith has empowered and guides her on a path to eliminate global poverty.

Years ago, Deborah attended a meeting about the reality of poverty and microfinance. She heard the story of a basket weaver from Bangladesh who had to borrow money from a moneylender to buy the materials for her products and would only be paid two pennies for all her work. However, if she just had twenty-five cents, she could start buying the materials on her own and recouping all the profits. This was the inspiration of microloans. Through small loans, people's financial circumstances could be dramatically transformed.

During a trip to Nepal, Deborah met a woman, who through a microloan borrowed $4—a sum this woman had never seen in her life. With that money she bought a comb, a pair of scissors, and a mirror, and she put her husband in business as a barber. Now she has a home, and her children are in school—all because of Deborah's $4.

Microfinance became Deborah's mission and passion, grounded in her belief that a community of people, all doing a little, could together have a huge impact. She founded the Foundation for Women and has funded programs in India, Zambia, South Africa, Niger—and Foundation for Women has operated a program in Liberia since 2006 and in the United States for a decade.

The change that Deborah's work has brought to families around the world certainly feels like a miracle. Her work is beyond hand-outs, and it has had a miraculous impact on countless lives and communities. Deborah believes we can make a difference, even if it's lending someone as little as twenty-fve cents. We can learn from Deborah to believe that we have a very important choice now; we must hold hands together to make a future.

Deborah is the author of *Gratitude Always: A Woman's Journey to Total Trust in Spirit,* in which she acknowledges that in our journey in life "some losses are necessary" but that we must get up every day to continue to follow God's calling for our lives. She believes that "Divine Spirit is guiding our steps; we are not alone if we ask for help. Anything is possible if we surrender to Spirit; [and] that celebrating this connection opens unbelievable possibilities."

> *May we believe, like Deborah, that we are never alone; the Spirit is guiding our steps, holding us in the darkest moments, celebrating our joys in the brightest light; holding hands with Spirit is the only way; and without this connection nothing is possible but with it, the possibilities are endless. Amen.*

Marie Fortune

1951–

Faith beyond Darkness

My faith gives me a way to experience the world in all its sadness and contradictions, and with all its suffering, and still know that God is good.

Marie Fortune has had a love/hate relationship with the church's "long-standing denial of women's ministries and ordination." Why did she stay? Because "Jesus came to bring us abundant life. Our job is to manifest that faith, hope and love as we live with our neighbors."

Many of us feel challenged by how to connect with the true and beautiful aspects of our faith amid the dark, swirling contradictions that can exist within religious institutions. But somehow, Marie has a solid grasp of both aspects of the tradition. She speaks out against oppression and exploitation within the church without condemning it or abandoning her love of God.

An ordained United Church of Christ pastor and author of several books, Marie works tirelessly to empower women, religiously and personally. A founder of the Women's Funding Alliance, formed to help women and girls triumph over domestic violence, Marie also served on the National Advisory Council on Violence against Women. She also served on the Defense Task Force on Domestic Violence with the US Defense Department.

Marie feels that Jesus's message to women suffering oppression and brutality is clear: "You are valued in God's eyes; your whole self is regarded by God as a temple, a sacred place. Just as God does not want a temple defiled by violence, neither does God want you to be harmed." And all spiritual leaders have a sacred obligation to teach nonviolence to their members and to take a more active role in ending domestic violence. Marie asserts that when the body is abused, so, too, is the soul. Therefore, it is exceedingly appropriate that houses of worship open their doors as spaces of healing.

Though she admits that the church is slow to change, it also lifts up the justice Jesus sought, and by extension, the imperative to effect change in the world. "Denying ourselves the spiritual resources of our traditions does nothing to change patriarchy. It just impoverishes us." This crucial distinction has birthed in Marie a fierce form of faith—one that does not collapse when the church fails in some way. Rather, it is in the seemingly darkest moments that Marie's faith ignites. Marie's capacity to call out the truth is a beacon to all who want to embrace both the limits and the glory of their faith.

> *Kind and loving God, may my faith strengthen my ability to call out injustices when I see them, aligning my heart with the sacred heart of Jesus, whose love connects us all. Amen.*

Anne Lamott

1954–

———

Sacred Tears

My faith is not a beautiful, glimmering faith.
It is based on desperation and doubt.

In those humbling moments when life knocks the wind out
of us, Anne Lamott's words can be a source of solace. She knows,
firsthand, how much life can hurt. Because Anne has experienced
this darkness, we trust her with our own pain and uncertainty.

A best-selling author of fiction and nonfiction alike, Anne has
lived from the shut-down place of drowning her pain in alcohol,
drugs, and eating disorders. Firmly entrenched on this path of self-
destruction, one morning Anne found herself sitting in church,
drawn to the singing: "Something inside me that was stiff and rot-
ting would feel soft and tender. Somehow the singing wore down
all the boundaries and distinctions that kept me so isolated. . . .
the music was breath and food."

Unfortunately for Anne, however, who was raised to question
religion, the idea of becoming Christian "seemed an utterly impossible thing that simply could not be allowed to happen. I turned
to the wall and said out loud, I would rather die."

Luckily God didn't heed this request! Instead of dying, Anne
became a Christian and opened herself to church, which gave
her the fortitude to open herself to the aching beauty of life.
Ultimately, she reminds us that no matter what life throws at us,

"you come through, and you learn to dance with the banged-up heart." Embracing our pain is part of the process that allows us to truly feel our own hurts and the hurt around us. In a society that puts a premium on "having it all together," Anne reminds us of the power of our tears:

> Promise you won't stop crying. Crying cleanses you. Waters of grief help you find your way home. Water helps you find your way into your own heart, and into the hearts of others. Crying baptizes you.

The price we pay for looking like we have it all together is a hard, brittle shell that hides the hurt underneath. Crying is the lubricant that softens the hard shell. It opens our hearts to the loving faith of Jesus and Mary. Only by being vulnerable can we truly discover ourselves. "The work of restoration is largely about remembering who you are."

Though it has, at times, been a brutal road for Anne, the more she surrenders, the more gifts she receives. Profound appreciation, for the deceptively simple things is one of the gifts that occurs when Anne allows herself to really settle into her life:

> Gratitude, not understanding, is the secret to joy and equanimity. I prayed for the willingness to have very mild spiritual well-being. I didn't need to understand the hypostatic unity of the Trinity; I just needed to turn my life over to whoever came up with redwood trees.

> *Merciful God, I pray for the ability to revel in the baptismal of my own tears. To embrace my pain, and to turn my life over to You, who made manifest the aching beauty of this world. Amen.*

Fighting Your Way Back

On the day I was born, I think God reached down and said, "Baby girl Annie, I am going to give you a good brain and some artistic talent and a sense of humor, but I'm also going to give you low self-esteem and hat hair, because I want you to fight your way back to me.

Intimately acquainted with the paralysis of self-doubt, Anne grows "anxious on my way to the dump with a car full of garbage, convinced that my garbage and I will be rejected . . . because it is so disgusting that the people who run the dump wouldn't want it." Anne knows well the feeling of giving up in despair. Though she allowed herself to sink into this well, she never lost hold of the rope God offered—a rope that always gave her the strength to fight her way back.

Our self-defeating attitudes are like quicksand. Nothing is more detrimental to our well-being. And the more we struggle, the more we seem to sink. "Your sick worried mind," Anne cautions, "can't heal your sick worried mind." So, when Anne is neck-deep in this personal quagmire and wants only to "stay home and sit on the couch, necking with my fear and depression," what brings her back? "When I am coming apart like a two-dollar watch, it helps me beyond words to look at myself through the eyes of Mary, totally adoring and gentle."

Anne has a widespread following because her writing taps into the universal experience of apathy and despair. Fortunately, she also lifts up in her writing what it takes to turn the corner. No matter how dark the depression, how bleak tomorrow looks, faith comes from being able to pull ourselves up from the floor. God never gives up on us, and is always willing to lend a helping hand. "God," Anne assures us, "has extremely low standards."

And in this sense, not taking ourselves too seriously is crucial to making this journey back intact. Anne writes about the perils of self-despair not only with unflinching honesty but a large dollop of humor. She makes us laugh because she knows the power that laughter brings: "I laughed so hard that it broke up the thin candy shell of fear that was covering my heart, and I could breathe again. I think that's what they mean by grace—the divine assistance for regeneration."

So, does this roller coaster ride of self-loathing, sinking in despair, stuffing ourselves with chocolate, fighting to find the sunlight of our faith again, before hitting another bout of self-loathing, ever come to an end? According to Anne, it does: "I have grown old enough to develop radical acceptance. I insist on the right to swim in warm water at every opportunity, no matter how I look, no matter how young and gorgeous the other people on the beach are. . . . On the day I die, I want to have had dessert."

> *My Lord, I am so weary of the constant fight within me. Let your love and divine acceptance be my guiding light, that I may develop radical acceptance of myself, and transform my judgment of others into compassion. Amen.*

Rita Nakashima Brock

1950–

Ecclesia

To be loved even when we do not know we are being loved is the power of ecclesia in our lives: to be called out by those who care.

As an adult, Rita Nakashima Brock found out about a life-altering family secret. She embraced this new discovery, which ultimately surrounded her in ecclesia, the community called by God. A well-known professor and speaker in feminist theology, some of Rita's most powerful images of God are drawn from these powerful personal experiences.

Rita was born in Japan, the daughter of a Japanese mother and a US serviceman. They moved to the United States when she was six. Many years later, after both her father and mother had died, Rita learned that she had a Puerto Rican biological father. When she went to look for him in San Juan, she discovered a large extended family who had been waiting many years to see her. They welcomed her with open arms. She learned that her grandfather had prayed every night before bed that he would meet his first grandchild before his death. Her grandmother had not prayed. She knew God would arrange for her to one day meet this granddaughter, whom she loved deeply despite knowing her only through the faded baby pictures she kept on her mirror.

For Rita, this new familial community, who loved her and prayed for her without ever having met her, embodies the image of God. It participates in ecclesia. As Rita explains, "Ecclesia means to call out, to summon together into an assembly. It is grounded in the Christian confession that God is love and we are to love one another." Ecclesia is both the community called out by God to embody God's love in the world and the community that, in turn, calls us out to do the same.

By forming communities that seek justice and wholeness for people and the earth, we reflect the image of God for generations to come. We love both those people we know and those we do not, as others before us have done. Rita reminds us, "For each of us there have been thousands of people, over many centuries and across many miles, who have loved us without knowing us, hearts unsung, unseen. Their hopes and dreams for the future, and their hard grittiness that clings to life against all odds, keep life going as they hold fast to the bonds of love and care."

As we bear the image of God in community, according to Rita, we find "God here, and here, and here, ecclesia." We receive in gratitude God's love, our inheritance from others who have gone before, others who, like Rita's grandparents, have prayed for us and longed for our arrival without yet knowing us. This is a love based not on our deserving, but on sheer grace. And, as Rita invites us, "through our hopes and dreams, through our holding to life against all odds, we too pass on this legacy of loving those who will never know us."

Gracious God, call me out to be your agent of love to the world. Embolden me to leave a legacy of hope and caring even for those whom I will never know. Amen.

Experiencing Suffering

The past and its traditions must liberate and make whole the present.

Drawing on her Japanese Buddhist roots and her work as a Christian scholar, Rita Nakashima Brock visions an Asian American theology that beautifully intertwines Asian culture and Western Christian thought. Common among these faith traditions is the attempt to address universal human suffering:

We must seek to embrace and acknowledge our own suffering and the suffering of all creation to bring healing to our broken world . . . Asian American women often express this embrace of suffering in images of the cross, not as substitutionary death or self-sacrifice, but as the image of solidarity, of how God suffers with us and of what it means to suffer with one another.

Acknowledging that much of this wording is Western Christian language, Rita knows that the truth lifted up is in the Buddhist tradition as well. Both deliver the message that we should not only embrace suffering but "experience and acknowledge it—before it can be healed . . . Denial of suffering severs life-giving connections to others and denies our experiences of the interdependence of all existence."

"In our pain," Rita maintains, "is the power of self-knowledge that brings us to a healing wisdom and compassion." Within indigenous Japanese practices she finds an embodied spirituality that enables many Asian American women to affirm their own experience of incarnation; one that carries them from suffering to healing. Within this experience lies their ability to "seek an intuitive nonlinear whole. That whole involves a sensitive attunement to my own inner subjective world as a source of compassionate healing of suffering."

The only way out is through. By bringing us the Asian understanding of acceptance as a powerful choice enabling us to move through our suffering, rather than a condoning of suffering and its causes, Rita shows us a door into the peaceful center of our own being where we are met with Divine love and mercy.

Loving Creator, help me to open my heart and accept suffering as part of the rhythm of life. In this loving embrace, let pain be transformed into compassion, healing, and wholeness. Amen.

Kwok Pui-Lan

1952–

~

Christianity along the Boundaries of Difference

Theology in the 21st century must inspire, provoke, and move us into prophetic action to address the global issues in the world. What does the good news of Jesus Christ mean for the homeless and marginalized? Unless we have come to know God in embodied ways, we will miss the fullness of the Gospel and God's overflowing love for creation.

Kwok Pui-Lan knows what it is like to live on the boundary. As a former citizen of Hong Kong, she lived in a colonized country—a Chinese woman under British rule. And as an Asian Christian, she knows what it feels like to be marginalized in global Christian dialogue. However, these periphery experiences have brought with them a gift. "Claiming a boundary existence, I have come to understand that marginality should not be seen as a curse, but should be cherished and celebrated as an invitation to many possibilities." She uses her experience of marginality to begin to explore the ways in which Christianity is shaped in the interaction of Asian culture and biblical understanding.

The introduction of the Bible into Asian culture is fraught with difficulty because "Asian countries have their own religious and cultural systems . . . Asian Christians have recognized the dissonance between the kind of biblical interpretation we have inherited and the Asian reality we are facing. We have to find new images for our reality and make new connections between the Bible and our lives."

Pui-Lan uses the term "dialogical imagination" to describe how "Asian theologians have combined the insights of biblical themes with Asian resources." She says dialogical imagination "operates not only in using the cultural and religious traditions of Asia, but also in the radical appropriation of our own history. We begin to view the history of our people with the utmost seriousness in order to discern the signs of the time and God's redeeming action in that history. We have tried to define historical reality in our own terms and find it filled with theological insights."

But she warns that "while the creation of a new narrative discourse of Christianity through the use of Asian idioms and stories may be a sincere attempt on the part of Asian theologians, it can be seen as yet another incidence of trying to fit local histories into the global design of Christianity, if it does not self-consciously challenge imperialistic impulses."

"We must claim back the power to look at the Bible with our own eyes," Pui-Lan asserts, "and to stress that the divine is within us, not in something sealed off and handed down from almost two thousand years ago . . . the critical principle lies not in the Bible itself but in the community of women and men who read the Bible and who through their dialogical imagination appropriate it for their own liberation."

> *Loving God help me to see the many ways which Your*
> *word may be interpreted to liberate and create a fuller*
> *understanding of Your presence in the world. Amen.*

Hyun Kyung Chung

1956–

In Solidarity and Love

*I want to do theology in solidarity with and in love for
my mother.*

At age thirty-two, after her parents had died, Hyun Kyung
Chung learned a dark family secret that irrevocably changed the
entire course of her life. The woman she'd thought was her mother
was not. Somewhere in Korea, there was another woman whose
soft voice had soothed Hyun Kyung throughout the first year of
her life. This voice had been silenced in Hyun Kyung's life for
three decades.

Hyun Kyung's father, well placed in Korean society and frustrated with his barren wife, found a lowly single mother to birth
a child for him. Hyun Kyung learned about this from her cousin
and went on a search for her birth mother, a search that transformed her life.

On finally finding her mother, she learned that her mother
had bonded with her that first year and that when "they took me
from my mother on my first birthday. . . . [she] did not want to
let me go." Because "women who give birth out of wedlock are
ostracized," Hyun Kyung's mother lost her community. And in
losing her daughter, she became distraught. Knowing that her
daughter would share her shame, she placed the small child in the
new parents' arms without protest.

The only way Hung Kyung's birth mother could reconcile her actions was by "erasing her very existence as a human being and pretending that I had not been born from her womb." Doing so led to great suffering, and Hyun Kyung's mother struggled with depression after this. Listening to "my mother's life story—her struggle for mere survival in this unfriendly world—I was angered by 'the culture of silence' in which she lived. People around her silenced her in every way. Without any system of support to be a productive and public person, the only way she could survive without being mutilated was by becoming totally invisible."

As Hyun Kyung reconnected with her mother "I felt something in my deepest being was broken open. . . . Through this ill, seventy-two-year-old woman . . . I felt that I was encountering the power of the despised in my people's history." This experience transformed Hyun Kyung's thoughts about theology. "I felt an inner powerful spirit turning me from my wish to do theology like Europeans and toward the open arms of my mother . . . my sovereign mother looked like an icon of God, through which I could clearly see what God was telling me about my mission."

A Professor of Theology at Union Seminary in New York, and a member of the International Peace Committee, Hyun Kyung's teachings inspire her students to give voice to their own, personal theology. Because Hyun Kyung knows that it is "our personal stories of agony and joy, struggle and liberation" that speak the theology of our hearts. Meeting her mother showed Hyun Kyung that the true theology of her heart was one that beat in solidarity with the silenced and marginalized. As Christians, Hyun Kyung believes, "We are following Jesus' vision of the Kingdom of God, the 'feast of the equals.' That is a radical vision of peace and justice for everyone, because we share the same gifts, the love of God, the fullness of life."

Dearest Jesus, help me to empower myself and others to seek a radical vision of peace, to bring the voices of all your people to the feast of equals, entrusting my faith to You as I labor in Your service. Amen.

Katica Nikolic

1961–

⌒

Bound Together

We must let go of an individual destiny and see the progress of our own soul in the destiny of others. We must learn that our future is bound together.

Each day, Dr. Katica Nikolic witnessed the enormous stress put on individuals and families from the genocidal war that ripped apart the former Yugoslavia in the 1990s. She served for four years as the only doctor for 294 prisoners of war, during which time she developed a specialization in posttraumatic stress disorder (PTSD). "I never left during the war," said Dr. Katica (as she is known). "I worked in the war hospital and clinic in [the central Bosnian town of] Prozor for 3½ years. I had around 4,500 patients." She had such focused commitment that the record indicated she once worked for ten straight days without sleeping.

Although Dr. Katica was born in Kiev in the former Soviet Union and grew up in Odessa, she considers herself a Catholic Croat Bosnian. She attended medical school in Belgrade, received her neuropsychiatry degree in Sarajevo and Zagreb, and settled eventually in the Rama area of central Bosnia. She says that she specializes in PTSD not only as a doctor but also as a victim. "One day I walked from the surgery room, too tired to take off my bloody shirts," she recalled. "I fell into a deep sleep on the floor before they came looking for me—there was another emergency. When they woke me up, I didn't know who I was." She realized that she was now suffering from trauma, just as her patients were.

Near the end of the war, she recalls a Muslim man approached her on the street to thank her. "I was embarrassed," she said, "because I didn't remember him." The man told her that she had saved the life of his son, who had been a driver for the medical center and was nearly beaten to death by Croat paramilitaries. Dr. Katica had risked her life to get him into the war hospital for treatment. Then she wrapped him in a gauze body wrap and smuggled him to safety.

Out of her experiences during the war, Dr. Katica cofounded Kuca Mira—the House of Peace—at the Franciscan monastery in the Rama valley. The center offers counseling and encourages prayer, art, and music in the healing process. "We must search for the small light of goodness in each other"—first by teaching people to accept themselves no matter what they did or experienced during the war, then helping them to accept others.

Dr. Katica believes that the creative combination of spirituality and psychology is the approach needed for Bosnia to be reborn. "We must let go of an individual destiny," she said, "and see the progress of our own soul in the destiny of others. We must learn that our future is bound together."

Oh God, open my eyes so that I can learn to truly see the divinity that resides in each one of us. Let me receive the lessons of Dr. Katica and learn to accept and love myself no matter what I've done or experienced. And help me to accept and love others. Amen.

Rose Marie Berger

1963–

⁓

Where God Is Found

The act of asserting our responsibility and relationship to a situation of oppression . . . creates emotional and spiritual space where it is possible for God to enter.

Rose Marie Berger was arrested for peaceful, prayerful protest against the Iraq war. She refused to stop praying outside the White House after her permit to demonstrate was revoked. A writer and editor for *Sojourners Magazine*, Rose shared of the almost four-hundred–strong multitude:

> I'm in a very mixed crowd of protesters on the verge of being arrested. We are a teeming mass of Pentecostals, pacifists, and pagans; Buddhist monks, Catholic priests, Jewish rabbis, and Katrina evacuees; anarchists, Gold Star moms, hip-hop preachers, and war vets. We are "rabble" in the ancient sense of the word—a "tumultuous crowd." And we are roused.

Kneeling on the pavement, Rose spent ten hours handcuffed within this "teeming mass." "It is always intensely clarifying to study scripture while surrounded by police armed with tasers, pepper spray, steel-tipped batons, and semi-automatic hand guns. The verses practically leap off the page." Her arrest brought alive for her not only the scriptures but Alice Walker's wisdom that "resistance is the secret of joy."

This experience was a defining moment for Rose, whose rich career in faith-based activism and pastoral leadership spanned more than two decades. She understood how deeply important chaos and rabble rousing are to manifesting God here on earth.

What Rose ultimately found in this "teeming chaos" was "God's redemption." God is so often found in those places that seem most abandoned by the institutional stamp of divinity. "The 'rabble' on the White House sidewalk were soaked in suffering and sin. The suffering of mothers who have lost sons in Iraq and Afghanistan; veterans with post-traumatic stress; and homeless hurricane evacuees with absolutely nothing left. The sin of those who have let go of their faith and the hypocrisy of those who claim peace, yet feel justified in demeaning anyone who disagrees with them."

Rose felt blessed to be allowed to view her sister and brother protesters through the compassionate eyes of God. This allowed her to see beyond the failure and sin to the soul beneath: "I realize that the hunger present here is much deeper and wider than a simple political message. These are people straining toward liberation. In the midst of the chaos I keep thinking, 'They are yearning to be free.'"

> *God, open my eyes as you did Rose Marie's that I may see the achingly beautiful humanity amid the chaotic rabble. Let me be a force of Your love here on earth. Amen.*

Kanyere Eaton

1965–

Transformative Freedom

Jesus likens himself to the shepherd who loves His sheep, gives His life for His sheep, saves His sheep and keeps His sheep forever. To follow Jesus is to love, give, save, and keep this love forever.

For women called to the ministry of word and sacrament, mentors are scarce and role models few and far between. Women often doubt the verity of that still, small voice that summons them to service. When Dr. Kanyere Eaton became the first woman to serve as pastor of the Fellowship Covenant Church in the 121-year history of this evolving New York congregation, she encountered a good deal of pushback.

Though the arduous selection process for a new senior minister resulted in a positive recommendation by the search committee, the idea of a female finalist sent the congregation into a tailspin. Some balled up her printed bio and threw it to the ground in anger. Others stormed out of the room. A cadre of naysayers circulated a petition, declaring their opposition to her candidacy, while those who were excited by the possibility of someone and something new kept their interest hidden behind masks of indifference.

The early months were trying. Senior officers resigned from their positions. The new Pastor Eaton was constantly challenged, heckled while she preached, circumvented when it came to making financial decisions, and undermined in meetings of the church board. One man turned his chair, so that his back faced her as she led worship service on Sunday mornings. Others ignored the long-standing black church tradition of referring to pastors with titular deference, choosing instead to refer to Rev. Eaton as "her," "Miss," or "Sister." But Kanyere knew that the daily indignities were par for the course for trailblazing women who step out of their places and into the pulpit.

Kanyere had prepared long and hard for this position, earning a Bachelor of Science degree from Cornell University, a Master of Science and Social Work degree from Columbia University, a Master of Divinity degree from Union Theological Seminary, and finally a Doctorate of Ministry degree from San Francisco Theological Seminary. And over time, through her efforts to educate and inspire Christ's church to grow into the measure of the full stature of Christ, she brought renewal and healing to her congregation.

Those who could not come to terms with the Reverend Pastor Eaton quietly took their leave. Many more, however, began to join. Men and women, and girls and boys joined themselves to the ministry. They came to be fed. They came to be loved. They came hoping to learn, to grow, and to be transformed. A new consciousness began to develop. Little children drew pictures of their pastor in the pulpit with lipstick and colorful robes. They learned early that women could lead in the church. Teen girls considered full-time ministry a viable career option after college. Male parishioners learned to defend the legitimacy of women in ministry to their more traditional friends. And adult women acknowledged that they too felt drawn to the task of feeding Christ's lambs. Today, six women serve as ministers and two left to plant their own churches. They saw a new model up close and realized that they could be it themselves.

Creator of all humankind, continue to pour out your Spirit on women and men and let gender justice roll down like mighty waters in your church and in all the world. Amen.

Serene Jones

1966–

—

The Grace of Risk

In that moment, standing in the darkness, I see anew,
life seems so perfect.

Jumping off the edge is part of the faithful life for Serene Jones. An ordained minister, a past president of the American Academy of Religion, and, since 2008, the first woman to serve as president of Union Theological Seminary in its 182-year history, she is also an avid risk-taker. This may seem a strange combination, but Serene's adventurous personality exists side by side with the grace of God in her life. Relying on "God as Ground" gives her the courage to live life at the margins, where she feels she is most needed.

"Believing in God drives you to ledges, propels you across boundaries, hurdles you into abysses, and leads you not just beside still waters, but into floods and torrential storms." In this way, answering God's call can lead us to the edge of our knowing. For Serene, this has often been a psychological ledge, where jumping off means leaving the security of her familiar life. Her trust in God enables her to move, willingly, into the unknown.

The ledge can be many things: a move, a challenging new job, or facing the death of a friend. Though not true for all of us, for Serene—who has spent significant time abroad—this ledge has sometimes meant being in situations that many would consider stressful or dangerous. During her seminary years, she went to India to witness the living conditions of the poor, and learn about the religious beliefs that shaped their lives. She later spent time among the underprivileged in the jungles of the Philippines. Always wanting to grow in understanding and faith, Serene insists that risk-taking is part of a healthy spirituality. "I jump off with the expectation that I will survive it, and will surface out of the waters with invigorating new life running down my face."

Reflecting on some of the risks she has taken, Serene recalls, "I had to leave the known and be open to letting something I hadn't mastered surprise me." She believes that when we stand at the brink of the scary and unknown, and decide in faith, to jump into it, we create an opening for God's grace, "a grace that undoes us, rupturing the given and tearing a hole in our lives that allows a future that is truly new to unfold."

Faithful risk-taking for Serene requires cultivating a "sensibility that one has to be radically open to transformation by a force that comes to us from outside ourselves." Although this means hurling oneself into the darkness, it also means that a steadfast God will be there to light our way.

> *Sustaining God, give me the courage to take risks that open up a new future for myself and others, trusting always that your grace will be there to greet me. Amen.*

Emily Nielsen Jones

1969–

⸺

Unfolding River

I would love to live like a river flows, carried by the
surface of its own unfolding.

—John O'Donohue

Emily Nielsen Jones's spiritual journey is that of constant unfolding and winding, leading her to become who she was truly meant to be. Growing up in a Protestant church she was frustrated by the all-male leadership. She began to feel trapped in a set of beliefs that did not respect her feelings. In her early thirties, she became a spiritual seeker having a very palpable sense that after three decades in this kind of church, there had to be another way. She experienced her own "contemplative awakening."

She allowed herself to become a beginner in the spiritual quest. During this time, she also became a mother. As she would hold her young babies, she had profound moments where she finally felt known, loved, and seen in raw form. It was a unitive knowing that reshaped this thing called "faith" that had been layered in imprinted beliefs from years of religious socialization. She began to claim a kind of spirituality that does not need to claim things as dogmatic and certain. Maybe there are realms that we can't see or contain with our mental structures. She became a woman of faith with roots in Christianity, but she could also live on the margins of the church, by relating to people as spiritual beings on a human journey.

Emily is the co-author of a project called *The Girl Child & Her Long Walk to Freedom: Putting Faith to Work through Love to Break Ancient Chains*, an e-book, website, and six-month reading journey that dives deeply into the religious and historical roots of patriarchy and systems of oppression. Emily's project brings awareness to the ugly truth of patriarchy in our history and society. It exposes tribal consciousness and shares the gruesome reality of abuse of women and girls. Emily sheds light on nightmare scenes, such as the way that girl babies were often killed in societies that valued boys more than girls. Her work supports people of faith to question the patriarchal structures of their own religious traditions that have blunted the emancipatory capacity to live faith more freely.

She has worked with others to increase access for women and girls in education, health, and the economy, so that they can reach their full potential. She works to address human rights issues for women and girls including sex trafficking, slavery, and gender-based violence, as well as supporting refugees.

Emily's life is an example of letting things evolve and unfold as a river on our own spiritual journey. She shows that with faith and trust, God's guidance will lead each of our lives through circumstances that can enrich and deepen our spirituality and the work we do in the world. We share a common humanity, and our faith inspires us to do all we can to "love our neighbor as ourselves" and do our part to make the world a little more kind and just.

May we, like Emily, entrust ourselves to the unfolding river of faith, and thus find God's plan for our lives. Amen.

Rachel Lloyd

1975–

~

From Pain to Life's Passion

*Every experience, every tear, every hardship has
equipped me for the work I do now. There is such a deep
satisfaction in knowing that I am fulfilling my purpose.*

Rachel Lloyd grew up an only child in Portsmouth, England. She never knew her father and dropped out of school at age thirteen to care for her alcoholic mother.

Though she began working in factories and restaurants, "it wasn't long before I found that there were easier ways to make money. My criminal endeavors earned me a lot of fast cash along with a police record." Rachel began drinking and doing drugs. Even with intervention, "I continued to slip through the cracks of a system that would eventually give up on me."

At age seventeen, Rachel was penniless and desperate. "I turned my first trick in a strip-club in Munich, while tears ran down my face, telling myself that I would simply do this until I could make enough money to go home." She was a prostitute for two years, "eventually getting out after my crack-addicted pimp tried to murder me."

Her slow journey back to health began when Rachel found her way into a German church home "where people provided me with spiritual guidance and love . . . and the practical things that I needed." Armed with strong female role models, "housing, a job, clothes and the very basic necessities," Rachel "began to see that I had other skills and abilities that I never thought I had. I began to see a whole new me." In that moment, Rachel knew "I wanted to give back to these girls."

Three years later Rachel came to the United States "as a missionary to work with adult women coming out of prostitution." The focus of her work quickly changed: "I began to see girls in Rikers (a New York City jail) who would say they were 18, but were visibly not." Even the older prostitutes would approach Rachel, begging her to get the thirteen- and fourteen-year-old girls off the streets.

In January 1999, Rachel manifested her life's passion by founding the Girls Education and Mentoring Services (GEMS). "There remains a deep scar across the palm of my right hand," Rachel shares in the Director's Message on the GEMS website. "Seventeen stitches, a vivid reminder of the last fight with my pimp. It's a reminder that I almost didn't make it . . . It's what allows me to see beauty, worth and potential in each and every girl we serve." Rachel's mission is clear: "The Bible says 'To whom much is given, much is required.' I know that I was able to survive and I would be remiss not to give back." Through her faith, Rachel shares that "pain has become my passion."

> *God, I too have scars from experiences I would rather forget. Through Your love I pray that I can turn my pain into a passion to make life better not just for myself, but for others. Amen.*

Reclamations

> *When I was working with the girls, people would say they are loose, promiscuous, but I thought they were*

> *amazing girls and they were gems. They just need love,*
> *housing, employment to still be beautiful and precious.*

A smartly dressed, petite woman in her late twenties, former prostitute Rachel Lloyd began the Girls Education and Mentoring Services (GEMS)

> on my kitchen table with a borrowed computer and thirty dollars. Originally, I was just going out into the facilities and working with young women, one on one. I used to put girls on my couch when I had nowhere else for them to go. I was working with other programs, trying to find them referrals. But I knew very clearly in my heart that we needed a very specific place for a very specific issue.

With a mission "to educate, support, and empower young women who are at risk of sexual exploitation, abuse, and violence," GEMS now has its own office and three employees. Founded to ensure that these girls do have a voice among people with power, GEMS isn't interested in "just treating the girls from a victim perspective . . . we're looking for a strength-based perspective as well."

At a congregational briefing in 2004, Rachel talked about survivors of domestic sex trafficking, though she was also talking about herself: "It didn't just take putting on a suit and getting on the plane. It took years of struggle and surviving and fighting, through danger and life-threatening experiences of feeling that you didn't belong, that you didn't fit in, that you were stigmatized by society, and that no one will ever hear your voice."

Rachel sees the same personal struggle in the eyes of the girls she serves through GEMS, many of whom are considered "unredeemable" by those refusing to acknowledge the complex social roots of underage prostitution. The average age that girls enter into prostitution is twelve, and there are an estimated one hundred thousand to three million adolescents in America who get involved in prostitution annually. But many schools deny the magnitude of this kind of child exploitation, preferring to believe that they "don't have that problem."

GEMS's success in working with these "unredeemable" girls is the authenticity and emotional availability of the staff and their respect of the girls they serve. They believe that each girl's "experiences have actually made [her] an expert."

Rachel's openness about her own journey encourages the girls to find their essence. She reminds them that prostitution "is not who you are. This is not forever." She instills in them the belief "that there's a part inside of you that's going to go on."

God of all compassion, I know Your highest command is for authenticity. I don't have to be perfect to do Your work. I only have to be honest and have faith in You. Amen.

Sources

Note: *Many of the quotations are found in easily discoverable online sources. Here are other useful references.*

Amma Sarra, Amma Syncletica, and Amma Theodora: Laura Swan, *The Forgotten Desert Mothers: Sayings, Lives, and Stories of Early Christian Women* (New York: Paulist Press, 2001; *The Sayings of the Desert Fathers: The Alphabetical Collection*, trans. Benedicta Ward (Kalamazoo, MI: Cistercian Publications, 1975); Benedicta Ward, *The Sayings of the Desert Fathers* (Kalamazoo, MI: Cistercian Publications, 1975).

Fabiola: All quotations from Letter LXXVII from St. Jerome to Oceanus, detailing the eulogy St. Jerome offered at Fabiola's funeral, http://www.newadvent.org/fathers/3001077.htm.

Hildegard of Bingen: Sabina Flanagan, *Hildegard of Bingen: A Visionary Life* (New York: Barnes & Noble, 1990).

Marguerite Porete: Robert Lerner, *Women Writers of the Middle Ages: A Critical Study of Texts from Perpetua to Marguerite Porete* (Cambridge: Cambridge University Press, 1984); Marguerite Porete, *The Mirror of Simple Souls*, trans. Ellen L. Babinsky (New York: Paulist Press, 1993).

Julian of Norwich: Julian of Norwich, *Revelations of Divine Love*, trans. Barry Windeat (Oxford: Oxford University Press, 2015).

Teresa of Avila: St. Teresa of Avila, *Interior Castle*, trans. and ed. E. Allison Peers (New York: Image/Doubleday, 1989); Victoria Lincoln, *Teresa, a Woman: A Biography of Teresa of Avila* (Albany: SUNY Press, 1984); Tessa Bielecki, *Holy Daring: An*

Outrageous Gift to Modern Spirituality from Saint Teresa, the Grand Wild Woman of Avila (Rockport, MA: Element, 1994); J. Mary Luti, *Teresa of Avila's Way* (Collegeville, MN: Liturgical Press, 1991).

Anne Hutchinson: Jay Rogers, "America's Christian Leaders: Anne Hutchinson," http://www.forerunner.com/forerunner/ X0193_Anne_Hutchinson.html; Anne Hutchinson Trial Transcription, Pt. 11, http://www.annehutchinson.com/anne_ hutchinson_trial_011.htm.

Mary Dyer: http://sites.rootsweb.com/~nwa/dyer.html.

Jeanne Mance: Françoise Deroy-Pineau, *Canada: Portraits of Faith*. http://www.ccheritage.ca/biographies/jeannemance.php.

Sor Juana Inés de la Cruz: Juana Inés de la Cruz, "The Poet's Answer to the Most Illustrious Sor Filotea De La Cruz," http:// info-center.ccit.arizona.edu/~ws/ws200/fall97/grp10/sorjuana- word.html.

Kateri Tekakwitha: https://www.newadvent.org/cathen/14471a. htm; Claude Chauchetiere, S.J., *The Life of the Good Catherine Tekakwitha,* https://web.archive.org/web/20110725120943/ http://www.thelifeofkateritekakwitha.net/en/cc/chapter1.html; Rev. Pierre Cholonec, *Kateri Tekakwitha: The Iroquois Saint* (Merchantville, NJ: Evolution Publishing, 2012).

Sojourner Truth: *Journey Toward Freedom: The Story of Sojourner Truth*, by Jacqueline Bernard (New York: Feminist Press at The City University of New York, 1990); Sojourner Truth Speeches Menu, http://www.sojournertruth.org/Library/Speeches/De- fault.htm.

Lydia Maria Child: Joan Goodwin, "Lydia Maria Child," https:// uudb.org/articles/lydiamariachild.html.

Maria W. Miller Stewart: Marilyn Richardson, *Maria W. Stewart: America's First Black Woman Political Writer* (Bloomington: Indiana University Press, 1988).

Harriet Beecher Stowe: www.HarrietBeecherStoweCenter.org.

Elizabeth Cady Stanton: *The Woman's Bible* (Mineola, NY: Dover Publications, 2003); Helen LaKelly Hunt, *And the Spirit Moved Them: The Lost Radical History of America's First Feminists* (New York: Feminist Press, 2017).

Frances Jane (Fanny) Crosby: https://believersweb.org/Frances-Jane-Crosby,-1820—1915/.

Mary Slessor: "Mary Slessor: The White Queen of Calabar," by Eugene Myers Harrison, ed. Stephen Ross, https://www.wholesomewords.org/missions/bioslessor2.html.

Sister Blandina Segale: Blandina Segale, *At the End of the Santa Fé Trail* (Milwaukee: Bruce Publishing, 1951).

Mary Jane McLeod Bethune: *Mary McLeod Bethune: Building a Better World*, ed. Audrey Thomas McCluskey & Elaine M. Smith (Bloomington: Indiana University Press, 1999).

Evelyn Underhill: Evelyn Underhill, *The Ways of the Spirit*, with introduction by Grace Adolphsen Brame (New York: Crossroad, 1990); *Evelyn Underhill: Essential Writings,* ed. Emilie Griffin (Maryknoll, NY: Orbis Books, 2003).

Aimee Semple McPherson: *This Is That: The Experiences, Sermons, and Writings of Aimee Semple McPherson,* ed. Douglas Harrolf (CreateSpace, 2016).

Dorothy Day: *Dorothy Day: Selected Writings,* ed. Robert Ellsberg (Maryknoll, NY: Orbis Books, 2005); Jim Forest, *All Is Grace: A Biography of Dorothy Day* (Maryknoll, NY: Orbis Books, 2011); Robert Coles, *Dorothy Day: A Radical Devotion* (Reading, MA: Perseus Books, 1987).

Anne Morrow Lindbergh: Anne Morrow Lindbergh, *Gift from the Sea* (New York: Pantheon Books, 1955).

Peace Pilgrim: *Peace Pilgrim. Her Life and Work in Her Own Words*, compiled by some of her friends (Santa Fe, NM: Ocean Tree Books, 1991).

Simone Weil: Simone Weil, *Waiting for God* (New York: G.P. Putnam's Sons, 1951); *Simone Weil, Essential Writings*, selected with an introduction by Eric O. Springsted (Maryknoll, NY: Orbis Books, 1998).

Rosa Louise Parks: Vincent F. A. Golphin, "Taking a Seat for Justice," *Christianity Today* 39, no. 5 (April 24, 1995).

Etty Hillesum: Etty Hillesum, *An Interrupted Life and Letters from Westerbork,* with a foreword by Eva Hoffman (New York: Henry Holt, 1996).

Fannie Lou Hamer: Kay Mills, *This Little Light of Mine: The Life of Fannie Lou Hamer* (New York: Dutton, 1993).

Madeleine L'Engle: Sarah Arthur, *A Light So Lovely: The Spiritual Legacy of Madeleine L'Engle* (Grand Rapids, MI: Zondervan, 2018).

Letty Russell: Letty M. Russell, *Church in the Round: Feminist Interpretations of the Church*, (Louisville, KY: Westminster John Knox Press1993); Margaret Farley and Serene Jones, eds. *Liberating Eschatology: Essays in Honor of Letty M. Russell* (Louisville, KY: Westminster John Knox Press, 1999).

Elizabeth O'Connor: Elizabeth O'Connor, *Call to Commitment: An Attempt to Embody the Essence of the Church* (Washington, DC: Church of the Savior, 2020).

Maya Angelou: Maya Angelou, *I Know Why the Caged Bird Sings* (New York: Random House, 2002); *Conversations with Maya Angelou,* ed. Jeffrey M. Elliot (Jackson: University Press of Mississippi Press, 1988).

Dorothee Soelle: *Dorothee Soelle: Essential Writings,* selected with an introduction by Dianne L. Oliver (Maryknoll, NY: Orbis Books, 2006).

Anne Frank: Anne Frank, *The Diary of a Young Girl:* with an introduction by Eleanor Roosevelt (New York: Bantam Books, 1993).

Maura Clarke: Ellen Markey, *The Assassination of Sister Maura* (New York: Bold Type Books, 2016); Judith M. Noone, MM, *The Same Fate as the Poor* (Maryknoll, NY: Orbis Books, 1995).

Beverly W. Harrison: Beverly W. Harrison, *Making the Connections: Essays in Feminist Social Ethics*, ed. Carol S. Robb (Boston: Beacon Press, 1985).

Audre Lorde: Audre Lorde, *The Cancer Journals* (San Francisco: Aunt Lute Books, 1980).

Cho Wah Soon: Cho Wah Soon, *Let the Weak Be Strong* (Bloomington, IN: Meyer-Stone Books, 1988).

Mercy Amba Oduyoye: Mercy Amba Oduyoye, *Daughters of Anowa: African Women and Patriarchy* (Maryknoll, NY: Orbis Books, 1995); *Beads and Strands: Reflections of an African Woman on Christianity in Africa* (Maryknoll, NY: Orbis Books, 2004).

Rosemary Radford Ruether: Rosemary Radford Ruether, *Sexism and God-Talk* (Boston: Beacon Press, 1983); *Gaia and God: An Ecofeminist Theology of Earth Healing* (San Francisco: HarperSanFrancisco, 1992).

Sister Joan Chittister: *Joan Chittister: Essential Writings,* ed., Mary Lou Kownacki and Mary Hembrow Snyder (Maryknoll, NY: Orbis Books, 2014).

Meinrad Craighead: Meinrad Craighead, *Crow Mother and the Dog God* (San Francisco: Pomegranate, 2003).

Suzanne Radley Hiatt: "Remembering Sue: Two Celebrations on the Life of Suzanne Radley Hiatt presented June 17, 2002 in St. John's Memorial Chapel," http://episcopalwomenscaucus.org/ruach/Fall2002_vol23_2_3/rememberSue.html; Mark Oppenheimer, "Episcopal Priestesses—Remembering the Philadelphia Eleven—Ordination of Women," *Christian Century*, Jan. 2, 2002, copyright 2002, Christian Century Foundation, copyright 2002 Gale Group.

Delores Williams: Delores S. Williams, *Sisters in the Wilderness: The Challenge of Womanist God-Talk* (Maryknoll, New York: Orbis Books, 1993).

Ann Ulanov: Ann Ulanov, *The Female Ancestors of Christ* (n.p.: Daimon, 1998).

Helen Prejean: Helen Prejean, *Dead Man Walking* (New York: Random House, 1993); *River of Fire: On Becoming an Activist* (New York: Random House, 2020).

Ita Ford: Jeanne Evans, ed. *"Here I Am, Lord": The Letters and Writings of Ita Ford* (Maryknoll, NY: Orbis Books, 2005).

Ivone Gebara: Ivone Gebara, *Longing for Running Water: Ecofeminism and Liberation* (Minneapolis: Fortress Press, 1999),

Bernice Johnson Reagon: "Singing to Freedom, An Interview with Bernice Johnson Reagon," *Sojourners Magazine* (August 2004).

Elaine Pagels: Elaine Pagels, *Why Religion: A Personal Story* (New York: Ecco, 2020); Elaine Pagels, Interview by Bill Moyers, *NOW* (PBS, May 16, 2003), http://www.pbs.org/now/transcript/transcript_pagels.html.

Ada María Isasi-Díaz: Ada María Isasi-Díaz, *En La Lucha / In the Struggle* (Minneapolis: Fortress Press, 1993); *Mujerista Theology: A Theology for the Twenty-First Century* (Maryknoll, NY: Orbis Books, 1996).

China Galland: China Galland, *Longing for Darkness: Tara and the Black Madonna* (New York: Penguin, 1990).

Carter Heyward: Carter Heyward, *Redemption of God: A Theology of Mutual Relation* (Lanham, MD: University Press of America, 1982).

Diana Eck: Diana Eck, *Encountering God: A Spiritual Journey from Bozeman to Benares* (Boston: Beacon Press, 1993); *A New Religious America: How a "Christian Country" Has Become the Most Religiously Diverse Nation* (San Francisco: HarperSanFrancisco, 2001).

Hanan Ashrawi: Rose Marie Berger, "Tanks versus Olive Branches: An Interview with Hanan Ashrawi," *Sojourners Magazine* (February 2005).

Jane Kenyon: John H. Timmerman, *Jane Kenyon: A Literary Life* (Grand Rapids, MI: Wm. B. Eerdmans, 2002); Jane Kenyon, *Collected Poems* (Saint Paul, MN: Graywolf Press, 2005).

Julia Cameron: Julia Cameron, *The Artist's Way* (New York: Jeremy P. Tarcher/Putnam, 1992).

Adele Ahlberg Calhoun: Adele Ahlberg Calhoun, *Spiritual Disciplines Handbook: Practices that Transform Us* (Downers Grove, IL: IVP Books, 2015); *Invitations from God: Accepting God's Offer to Rest, Weep, Forgive, Wait, Remember, and More* (Downers Grove, IL: IVP Books, 2011).

Bernadette Cozart: Diann L. Neu, *Return Blessings: Ecofeminist Liturgies Renewing the Earth* (Glasgow: Wild Goose Publications, 2004); Melvin Delgado, *Community Social Work Practice in an Urban Context: The Potential of a Capacity-Enhancement Perspective* (New York: Oxford University Press, 1999).

Deborah Lindholm: Deborah Lindholm, *Gratitude Always: A Woman's Journey to Total Trust in Spirit* (CreateSpace, 2014).

Marie Fortune: Marie Fortune. *Keeping the Faith: Guidance for Christian Women Facing Abuse* (New York: HarperCollins Publishers, 1995).

Anne Lamott: Anne Lamott, *Traveling Mercies: Some Thoughts on Faith* (New York: Pantheon Books, 1999); *Plan B: Further Thoughts on Faith* (New York: Riverhead Books, 2005); *Operating Instructions: A Journal of My Son's First Year* (New York: Pantheon Books, 1993).

Rita Nakashima Brock: Rita Nakashima Brock, *Journeys by Heart: A Christology of Erotic Power* (New York: Crossroad, 1988).

Kwok Pui-Lan: Kwok Pui-Lan, "Discovering the Bible in the Non-Biblical World," in *Lift Every Voice: Constructing Christian*

Theologies from the Underside, ed. Susan Brooks Thistlethwaite and Mary Potter Engel (Maryknoll, NY: Orbis Books, 1998).

Hyun Kyung Chung: Hyun Kyung Chung, *Struggle to Be the Sun Again* (Maryknoll, NY: Orbis Books, 1990).

Katica Nikolic: Rose Marie Berger, "A Laboratory of Reconciliation," in *Sojourners Magazine* (November–December 1999), https://sojo.net/magazine/november-december-1999/laboratory-reconciliation?action=magazine.article&issue=soj9911&article=991121.

Rose Marie Berger: Rose Marie Berger, "Rabble Rousing," *Sojourners Magazine* (December 2005).

Serene Jones: Quotes from personal correspondence; *Call It Grace: Finding Meaning in a Fractured World* (New York: Viking, 2019).

Emily Nielsen Jones: "The Girl Child and Her Long Walk to Freedom," www.girlchildlongwalk.org.

Rachel Lloyd: https://www.gems-girls.org/.

Index of Entries